STANDARDS IN PRACTICE GRADES 3-5

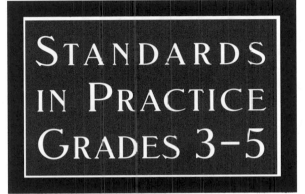

STANDARDS IN PRACTICE GRADES 3-5

MARTHA SIERRA-PERRY

WITH
JAN EWING
DEBORAH FOERTSCH
STEPHANIE SIERRA

National Council of Teachers of English
1111 W. Kenyon Road, Urbana, Illinois
61801-1096

Manuscript and Production Editor: Lee Erwin
Cover and Interior Design: R. Maul
Cover Photograph: Thompson-McClellan Photography
Interior Photographs: SLR Images (pp. 55, 85);
Thompson-McClellan Photography (pp. 8, 83, 86). Photograph on
p. 49 courtesy of International Business Machines Corporation.
"Keep a Poem in Your Pocket" (p. 18) is from *Something Special*,
by Beatrice Schenk de Regniers. Copyright © 1958, 1986 Beatrice Schenk
de Regniers. Reprinted by permission of Marian Reiner for the author.

NCTE Stock Number 46937-3050

It is the policy of NCTE in its journals and other publications to provide a forum for the open
discussion of ideas concerning the content and the teaching of English and the language arts.
Publicity accorded to any particular point of view does not imply endorsement by the Executive
Committee, the Board of Directors, or the membership at large, except in announcements of
policy, where such endorsement is clearly specified.

Although every attempt is made to ensure accuracy at the time of publication,
NCTE cannot guarantee that published electronic mail addresses are current.

Library of Congress Cataloging-in-Publication Data
Sierra-Perry, Martha, 1949–
    Standards in practice, grades 3–5 / Martha Sierra-Perry with Jan
Ewing . . . [et al.].
        p.   cm.
    Includes bibliographical references (p.   ).
    ISBN 0-8141-4693-7 (pbk.)
    1. Language arts (Elementary)–United States.   2. Language arts
(Elementary)–Standards–United States.   I. National Council of
Teachers of English.   II. Title.
    LB1576.S42   1996
    372.6'044–dc20   95-49756
                                                      CIP

FOREWORD

This book is one of four in the NCTE Standards in Practice series. The idea for this series grew out of requests from many teachers around the country who participated in the development of the NCTE/IRA standards and who asked if we could publish a book or a series of books that would illustrate what the standards might look like in actual classrooms at different grade levels.

This request was both inviting and challenging. Because one of the main goals of NCTE is to support classroom teachers, providing a series of books that would help define the standards seemed like the sort of thing we should do—and it is the type of thing, we like to think, we do quite well. At the same time, there were many challenges in developing these books. We wondered: Could we do it? What might these books look like? What standards would we use? How important would uniformity and consistency be among the books in the series?

The four authors and I spent time exploring these questions and it soon became evident that the development of this series was, perhaps, both simpler and even more important than we had originally thought. We decided that if we asked English language arts teachers who were doing interesting and challenging work in their classrooms to reflect in writing on their practices and to tell us their stories, the standards would be there, already at work in students' learning. After all, the English language arts standards did emerge from those practices that our membership and the IRA membership said they valued most. The standards do not stand above and apart from the practices of actual classroom teachers, or dictate to them—rather they represent what those teachers and the many others involved in English language arts education agree is the best and most productive current thinking about teaching and learning. We also decided that each book in the series did not have to follow the same generic format. What each book should do instead is tell its own story and use the format that best fits and supports the story or stories being told.

All of us agreed that we wanted the books in this series to be stories or rich illustrations of classroom practice. Stories, we thought, would allow the writers to capture the rich and complex activities of teaching and learning and, in addition, would illustrate the interconnectedness of the English language arts and of the standards themselves. We also wanted our readers to see how teachers create contexts as well as learning experiences. We thought it was important for the readers to experience both the struggles *and* the successes teachers and students encounter. And we hoped that the stories would make explicit the importance of the teacher as researcher. We believe the standards are dynamic in nature and will change and improve only if teachers actively and deliberately interrogate their own practice—learning and growing from their professional and classroom experiences.

In these four books we meet caring teachers who meet all our most challenging criteria for teaching and learning. They are women and men who think deeply about the quality of life and intellectual growth they provide for their students. Some of the teachers we meet in the series are new to the profession and are trying out ideas for the first time. Others have been teaching for many years but, as always, are reflecting on and questioning some of their practices, and in their stories we see them making changes. All of them, whether they are teaching five-year-olds or eighteen-year-olds, whether they themselves have been teaching for five or for eighteen or more years, put students' learning at the center of their curricula and engage their students in challenging, authentic experiences. By presenting an array of classroom portraits, these volumes clearly show that standards are always present in good practice and that there is no one way for the standards to be realized.

I want to commend the teachers and students who are featured in this series and the writers who told their stories. They have opened their classrooms to us and let us look in, and, in so doing, they have enriched our understandings of what matters most in the English language arts.

—Karen Smith
Associate Executive Director
National Council of Teachers of English

CONTENTS

NCTE/IRA STANDARDS FOR THE ENGLISH LANGUAGE ARTS

The vision guiding these standards is that all students must have the opportunities and resources to develop the language skills they need to pursue life's goals and to participate fully as informed, productive members of society. These standards assume that literacy growth begins before children enter school as they experience and experiment with literacy activities—reading and writing, and associating spoken words with their graphic representations. Recognizing this fact, these standards encourage the development of curriculum and instruction that make productive use of the emerging literacy abilities that children bring to school. Furthermore, the standards provide ample room for the innovation and creativity essential to teaching and learning. They are not prescriptions for particular curriculum or instruction.

Although we present these standards as a list, we want to emphasize that they are not distinct and separable; they are, in fact, interrelated and should be considered as a whole.

1. Students read a wide range of print and nonprint texts to build an understanding of texts, of themselves, and of the cultures of the United States and the world; to acquire new information; to respond to the needs and demands of society and the workplace; and for personal fulfillment. Among these texts are fiction and nonfiction, classic and contemporary works.

2. Students read a wide range of literature from many periods in many genres to build an understanding of the many dimensions (e.g., philosophical, ethical, aesthetic) of human experience.

3. Students apply a wide range of strategies to comprehend, interpret, evaluate, and appreciate texts. They draw on their prior experience, their interactions with other readers and writers, their knowledge of word meaning and other texts, their word identification strategies, and their understanding of textual features (e.g., sound-letter correspondence, sentence structure, context, graphics).

4. Students adjust their use of spoken, written, and visual language (e.g., conventions, style, vocabulary) to communicate effectively with a variety of audiences and for different purposes.

5. Students employ a wide range of strategies as they write and use different writing process elements appropriately to communicate with different audiences for a variety of purposes.

6. Students apply knowledge of language structure, language conventions (e.g., spelling and punctuation), media techniques, figurative language, and genre to create, critique, and discuss print and nonprint texts.

7. Students conduct research on issues and interests by generating ideas and questions, and by posing problems. They gather, evaluate, and synthesize data from a variety of sources (e.g., print and nonprint texts, artifacts, people) to communicate their discoveries in ways that suit their purpose and audience.

8. Students use a variety of technological and informational resources (e.g., libraries, databases, computer networks, video) to gather and synthesize information and to create and communicate knowledge.

9. Students develop an understanding of and respect for diversity in language use, patterns, and dialects across cultures, ethnic groups, geographic regions, and social roles.

10. Students whose first language is not English make use of their first language to develop competency in the English language arts and to develop understanding of content across the curriculum.

11. Students participate as knowledgeable, reflective, creative, and critical members of a variety of literacy communities.

12. Students use spoken, written, and visual language to accomplish their own purposes (e.g., for learning, enjoyment, persuasion, and the exchange of information).

INTRODUCTION

THE ART OF TEACHING

For several centuries, down through the many dynasties, a village was known for its exquisite and fragile porcelain.

Especially striking were its urns: High as tables, wide as chairs, they were admired around the globe for their strong form and delicate beauty.

Legend has it that when each urn was finished, there was one final step. The artist broke it, and then put it back together with gold filigree.

An ordinary urn was then transformed into a priceless work of art. What seemed finished wasn't....

In this book, you will meet four teachers—Deb Foertsch, Jan Ewing, Stephanie Sierra, and me, Martha Sierra-Perry. We are all different people, of course, who have different experiences, beliefs, and ways of knowing and teaching, and at the beginning of each chapter, you will learn more about us and what we do. What we have in common, however, is very important: we have seen for ourselves how taking another look at our philosophy and practice can transform us professionally in ways we would never have imagined possible. We hope that by joining us on the paths along which our journeys have taken us, you too will find new paths to follow, new ways of seeing, inquiring, and developing to your best potential. We offer ideas and strategies for you to try in your classrooms, and we hope you will "break" these ideas and expand upon them to make them your own through your art of teaching.

How do the NCTE/IRA Standards for the English Language Arts fit in? We see them as a guide developed by many of our colleagues, who relied upon a great deal of information from professional resources, input from colleagues and peers, and feedback from scores of teachers like you and me. We see them as a scaffold for us to rely upon as we build our professional knowledge and insights. We see them as a way to communicate with parents and the media so that we know all of us are working toward common goals for the benefit of all our students. We have a roadmap of sorts in the standards, which shows us our overall destination, but we still have the freedom to choose how we get there. The standards are not meant to confine us or our students. They are meant to offer paradigms that are both solid and flexible according to individual needs; they are built upon sound theory for us to rely upon in our own ways. In this book we show you how the standards can be translated into the different practices of four classrooms. We hope the material will offer you alternative ways of looking at, as well as confirmation of, your classroom practice, and we also hope that the book illustrates the common foundation underlying all good teaching and effective learning.

Of course, this means that we must continue to be open to change. which is most often easier said than done. We hope to provide models of how change took place within us, but we need to stress that change occurs very differently for different people.

How does a teacher begin to rethink the way he or she does things? A colleague may make a comment that the prescribed curriculum doesn't fit anymore—the comment rings true to us, and a subtle shift takes place in our minds. Parents may raise the question of whether the gifted program meets the needs of their children; they see a lot of worksheets but aren't sure how those worksheets are adding to their children's learning experience—inside we hear a faint voice that says perhaps they're right. Another subtle shift. Students themselves begin to question their learning—this is shown in the closed faces and glazed eyes of some children, the restlessness in others. We see that we're not reaching them somehow, and we wonder how some became so passive and some so afraid of failing that their natural curiosity is stymied. Could that have anything to do with us? Another shift.

We could choose to ignore those faint murmurings of dissatisfaction by reasoning them away—we're overworked and underpaid, and expected to be social workers as well as educators; there are too many parents who are too busy themselves trying to provide a living to have as much time as they would like for their children; new gimmicks and quick fixes in education come and go faster than the changing tide; and on and on and on. The fact is. no matter what reasons we come up with, we stay in the same dissatisfied place. And we and our students suffer for it. Recycling, revising, or revamping the curriculum without attending to the very real changes taking place in our society, and without attending to the changes needed in our thinking about student learning, leaves us feeling frustrated and defensive. What happened to the idealism we had in the beginning?

So we begin to look again. There is good news. The authors of the NCTE/IRA standards illustrate that the common perception of woeful educational progress in English and the language arts is ill-founded. We have actually done a pretty good job; our students are for the most part able to meet the basic standards of literacy called for by the critics, and meeting them more fully than before.

Many of us know, however, that the basics are not enough. The challenge for us is to help all of our students move toward a greater control of language so that they are able to participate fully in our increasingly complex, democratic, technological society. That's where our thinking differently about pedagogy and practice comes in, and it's often not easy.

In my own experience as a curriculum director, I found myself facing an explosion of discussion about what content should be taught, and how it should be taught. Many professional organizations were looking at and attempting to answer those same questions. In 1991, the National Council of Teachers of Mathematics released their standards, which gave us a model to refer to. The science profession looked at their organizing disciplines and began to dismantle their "layer-cake" approach to science education. The California Framework came to the forefront when teachers and curriculum leaders rejected all texts for history, since none in their professional opinion qualified for recommendation, and many of us were struck by the power of this action. This grassroots approach served as a model to the departments of education of other states and to school districts. Core to this whole evolution were the principles that guide our understanding of how children learn, and what is worth knowing.

The NCTE/IRA standards are grounded in principles that have emerged as a unifying consensus for teaching and learning across the disciplines. As Steven Zemelman, Harvey Daniels, and Arthur Hyde point out, "A progressive educational paradigm is strongly backed by educational research, draws on sound learning theory, and has under other names been tested and refined over many years" (1993, 7).

For years, many teachers have known intuitively what creates successful classroom experiences; now there is a wealth of research to support that intuitive knowledge, and teachers who know about that research are able to articulate why they do what they do. The combination of good instincts and thoughtful reflection is incredibly powerful, and the more we can talk about our reflections with others, the better.

The most valuable learning experiences are those that help students recognize learning as a natural process for pursuing personally meaningful goals and see themselves as determiners of their own success. Learning is socially mediated, as meaning is constructed from information and experience filtered through each individual's unique perceptions, thoughts, and feelings, and it becomes incumbent upon us as teachers to recognize and support what each student needs. Students are able to create knowledge from whatever data is available, able to organize information that links new information with previous knowledge in unique and future-oriented ways, and capable of "thinking about thinking." The key word is "capable." Instead of the teacher doing for the student, he or she provides engagements that tap into the learning process. What might those engagements look like? The stories in this book provide us with an opportunity to look directly into the classrooms of teachers who work hard to create and foster learning communities where children thrive in their own unique ways.

It would be very easy to accept the implied or overt labels that are often assigned to different students' performance abilities. But who is served by this practice? Certainly not the students. Instead, if we as teachers draw from our own experiences about when we were successful as learners, we realize that we were and continue to be our best when others believe that we are capable. It is imperative that we provide this belief for our students.

If we think about learner-centered instruction, we recognize that individuals proceed through identifiable progressions of physical, intellectual, and social development. In a learner-centered classroom, the teacher closely monitors where the student is in language and reading capabilities. As students approximate the appropriate learning or begin to demonstrate understanding, the teacher is there "just in time" to assist the student in making the next connection. Knowing that learning is developmental does not mean that we keep students from rich classroom experience. Instead, it means that we provide varied instruction and activity for our students—all of them. Sound teaching gives students opportunities to begin to construct the background information for literacy success; we aren't able to change our students' life experiences prior to their arrival in our classrooms, but we can take them from where they are and give them the support they need to reach the next step in their learning.

Of course, the classroom teacher is not the only one in the classroom who can help the students achieve. By recognizing that learning is facilitated by social interactions and by viewing social and cultural diversity as strengths, teachers can also help students learn to appreciate and help one another. In this way, many students who might otherwise be left out of the learning loop find a way to belong. They are accepted, and in turn this provides them with an opportunity to see others' potential and to have others see theirs. Adapting instruction to meet individual differences gives strength to all.

Learners differ in their unique capabilities in particular areas, and they differ in their learning modes and strategies. Creating a classroom that allows students to draw on their individual ideas, understandings, and developing beliefs in order to construct reality and interpret their life experience encourages them to be responsible for their learning.

The teachers in this book who invite you into their classrooms demonstrate these guiding principles as they develop, implement, and reflect upon the instructional strategies they put in place in those classrooms. Consequently, they also learn through their reflection. Just as learning is developmental for children, it is for adults as well. Administrators who give teachers time and permission to move on in their professional journeys enhance their own learning and that of the teachers through professional development, common planning, and a commitment to including teachers more coherently in developing the systems of governance at their schools. Learning results in change, and change occurs over time. We change at our own rates; "short cuts" and insensitive comparisons to the learning of other teachers will work against helping teachers develop to their best potential. The progress of each learner—whether it be teacher or student—should be compared only to that learner's own progress in achieving efficacy. The recognition of individual differences and the cognitive filters that we all use to structure our own learning must be respected. In environments of collegiality, collaboration, and mentoring, we can all become our best. And our students benefit because of that.

Our challenge is to break through our thinking and transform our classroom practice into artistry. We welcome you into our teaching lives and hope you will be inspired to create your own masterpieces.

Reference

Zemelman, S., Daniels, H., and Hyde, A. (1993). *Best practice: New standards for teaching and learning in America's schools.* Portsmouth, NH: Heinemann.

ACKNOWLEDGMENTS

First, I would like to thank Karen Smith for believing in teachers. Throughout the Standards in Practice project, Karen has been committed to showing that classroom teachers are creatively developing effective instruction with their students. The NCTE/IRA Standards for the English Language Arts serve as support to the best practices already going on in classrooms and open the conversation to other stakeholders. Next, I would like to thank Jan Ewing, who graciously stepped forward to further this project. Her professionalism is outstanding. Heartfelt thanks also to Dawn Boyer, Director of Acquisitions and Development in Publications, who kept the writers focused with her insightful editing and words of encouragement. Her positive attitude helped us to remain true to the vision of this project.

I would also like to thank my network of friends and colleagues: Stephanie and Deb for agreeing to work on this project; Dr. Margie Jobe, my son's emergency mom; Dr. Carmen Woods Chapman, who challenges my thinking; the teachers and administrators in Champaign Community Unit District #4, who shared their talents and worked to improve our curriculum; and the teachers at Jefferson Middle School and Centennial High School, who have given me opportunities to work on leadership and learning.

Finally, I would like to thank my family: my extended family, who cheer my successes and share my sorrows; my brothers and sisters, who are always there for me; and Ed and Nathanial, who have been so understanding, patient, and forgiving—I love you.

DEDICATION

"Leadership and learning are indispensable to each other."
–John F. Kennedy

To my mother and father, who through their love and leadership taught me to question the way things are in order to learn what I could do.

CHAPTER ONE

READING MORE INTO READING

When you meet Deb Foertsch, you know you've met a teacher who cares passionately about her work and her students' learning. There's a twinkle in her eye, a knowing look, a contagious laugh, and words that ring with enthusiasm and insight. "In the beginning," Deb says when referring to her growth as a professional, "which for me was seventeen years ago, there was the basal and boredom and fear. The fear of not teaching reading the 'right' way, the fear of losing control of the class, the fear of poor test results." Reading class in the beginning of Deb's career was fifty minutes long; other than being handed a teacher's manual, she received no information about what her students needed, and so this is how she proceeded:

1. Teacher introduces vocabulary on the chalkboard.
2. Students read basal story aloud, stopping periodically to answer teacher-asked "discussion questions."
3. Students write answers to questions at the end of the story and complete workbook pages correlated to the text.
4. Teacher checks students' work and assigns grades.
5. Class goes on to the next story.

Worse than the "ho-hum" feeling this routine gave Deb and her students was the feeling of frustration she experienced dragging the kids through each story and still not knowing whether they were becoming better readers. Deb began to ask herself questions: How *does* one become a better reader? How could she teach reading so that kids would *really* read, improve their writing abilities, and enjoy doing so? With those questions came the first steps of her journey toward improving reading instruction. She was initially looking for something *revolutionary*–"the answer." What she got instead was *evolutionary*–coming up with some answers but realizing that there was more power in pursuing the right questions.

Deb began by looking next door. Her colleague's class looked wonderful; the students were happy to be there, they were actively learning, and there was a sense of classroom "self-control" that she desperately wanted for her own class.

So she watched closely. She observed those students and that teacher, she continued to ask questions, and she began to modify what she saw to fit her students and herself. She began to create her own style. Then Deb decided to work on her master's degree. She wanted reading instruction to be the focus of her studies, because that's what she believed she most needed to improve. She became involved with the local reading council, went to workshops and conferences, and read. And read. And read. She read journals—*Reading Teacher, Language Arts.* And she read books by influential educators like Donald Graves, Lucy Calkins, and Regie Routman.

As she learned, Deb made changes in her reading instruction, in her concept of classroom organization, and in her attitudes toward her students and her beliefs about how children learn. She began to read aloud to students every day, and she was amazed at the level of thinking they expressed when they discussed the story along the way. She began to value student book selection and to listen, really listen, to students' ideas about literature and how they viewed themselves as learners. She began to uncover her strengths as a teacher and worked to put those strengths together with what she knew was important for students to learn and experience. And all of this listening and observing, learning and asking, trying and modifying has by no means ended. All of it has brought Deb to where she is now, which is why she feels it important to share her experiences and ideas with other professionals. She knows she has a long way to go, but it is her responsibility to offer what she can to help others like her along the way on their own journeys.

Here is a list of what Deb has come to believe about literacy instruction and learning:

Students learn best

- in a community of learners;
- in a safe environment;
- when reading, writing, speaking, and listening occur across the curriculum;
- when literacy instruction blends demonstration and explanation, guided and independent practice, teacher and student support, individual pursuits, student choices, and teacher direction; and
- when learning is student-centered, with hands, minds, and hearts engaged.

Deb teaches best when she

- respects students and herself;
- communicates with students, parents, and colleagues;
- acts on her belief that literacy is a way to think, and encourages it as a tool for understanding;
- keeps instruction "connected";
- focuses on helping students to become lifelong learners by providing experiences, formats, frameworks, and attitudes for study in the present and future;
- draws from all resources available;
- stresses process *and* product;
- provides equal access to literature, technology, learning opportunities, and herself;

- provides time to her students and herself for reflection and revision; and
- keeps a sense of humor.

Everyone benefits when
- creativity counts.

The way the classroom is now structured, the way the students are taught, encouraged, and evaluated, is grounded in these beliefs. Here, then, is how reading instruction now looks in Deb's room.

Reading as Exploration and Opportunity

Large-group instruction, flexible small-group instruction, daily independent reading, daily teacher read-aloud, daily "book boosts" and book sharing, and book "clubs" (just for fun) are all incorporated into the curriculum in Deb's classroom. Reading strategies and attitudes are demonstrated, supported, and practiced. Reading exploration is encouraged, and opportunities to read are always presented.

Large-Group Instruction: What It Looks Like

Deb feels strongly about introducing her students to quality literature. She reads the books herself before deciding whether they might be something the students will benefit from, and she uses criteria such as the author's use of language, a well-developed story, good character development, relevant subject matter that will help her students think in different ways about their world, and material that will touch her students' hearts. *Sing Down the Moon,* by Scott O'Dell, is one such book, and all students are given copies to read on their own and discuss in class together. (Deb obtains books for her classroom any way she can—whether through using points from publishers' book clubs, buying books herself, obtaining them through the PTA, or purchasing them through the school and school district.) Deb opens this particular lesson by asking, "If you were going to introduce Bright Morning to someone who had never read *Sing Down the Moon,* what words would you use to describe her?"

Hands fly into the air, followed by shouts of, "Pretty! Sad! Nice! Scared!" After a "one-at-a-time" reminder, students continue to offer descriptions, and Deb writes them on the overhead. After three minutes, Deb tells the class that the list needs to be narrowed down to the six descriptors that will tell the most about Bright Morning. She takes nominations from the floor, the class votes, and Deb circles the top six words. Then, using the first description on the narrowed-down list, Deb asks the students to find a place in their books that shows that Bright Morning "didn't give up, even though lots of people would've." In a minute, hands are in the air again. After calling on several students to read from their selections, Deb asks each to explain why he or she thinks a particular selection shows Bright Morning's strength of character. Students often respond to the question by saying that if they faced a similar situation they wouldn't give up, but most of the people they know probably would (ah, invincible fifth graders!). Next, it's time for some individual practice with small-group support. Deb assigns each group a different description from the shortened list, and each stu-

Students read a wide range of print and nonprint texts to build an understanding of texts, of themselves, and of the cultures of the United States and the world; to acquire new information; to respond to the needs and demands of society and the workplace; and for personal fulfillment. Among these texts are fiction and nonfiction, classic and contemporary works.

Students read a wide range of literature from many periods in many genres to build an understanding of the many dimensions (e.g., philosophical, ethical, aesthetic) of human experience.

dent is to find two different places in the book that illustrates the particular characteristic of Bright Morning. They mark the two places with stick-on notes (kept handy in their desks), and then write about:

1. How the chosen piece of text shows a particular characteristic.
2. Why that characteristic might be an important one to have or not to have in their own lives.

Deb requires students to work on their own for several minutes. She circulates during this quiet, busy time, noting in her mind who will need help later, but offering very little help at this point. It is important, she knows, to give them time to develop their own ideas. Students are then asked to share their marked places and written ideas with others in their groups, and to help others in the group who might be having a hard time. Deb circulates again during this work, this time stopping to help individuals and groups needing support. After it looks to her as though everyone has shared ideas and most are on the right track, she stops the class and asks them to fix up or change anything on their papers that they'd like to. "It's OK if you changed your mind about what you first wrote now that you've heard other group members' ideas," Deb says. "You can add on to your old ideas, change them around, or stick to what you had to begin with. It's important to listen to others' ideas and maybe change your mind about what you once thought. It's also OK to stick to what you first wrote down, if it shows your best ideas."

After several minutes of writing, Deb collects papers to review later. She knows that the class will look at characters in literature again and again throughout the school year, but these first papers will help her to gauge how individuals progress with their understanding of how an author reveals character. The papers will also tell her how much support certain students will need with revisiting the text and thinking about their reading.

Large-Group Instruction: Why It Looks That Way

Deb knows that thinking about how an author writes to make a character "come alive" in a piece of literature is a strategy that may be challenging to many fifth graders. It's an important strategy, however, not only because it encourages students to examine the text more closely in an evaluative way, but also because it can be a useful aid in strengthening characterization in their own writing. The book *Sing Down the Moon* was also important to the themed social studies unit the class was exploring, which is another reason Deb chose to use whole-class instruction for this lesson.

Deb uses large-group (or, in her case, "whole-class") instruction periodically throughout a reading theme. Whole-class literature experiences are important for establishing a sense of community, for creating a classroom's "language" and common frame of reference. For example, students will refer to their experience with this book when they read other titles and make connections—"That's just like in *Sing Down the Moon;* they were forced out of their homeland too." Deb wants the whole class together when a new theme is introduced, when a reading strategy that is new or difficult for most of the students is discussed, when especially challenging ideas or vocabulary is talked about, when students share or refine their ideas, and when they reveal their favorite passages, poems, or books.

Students participate as knowledgeable, reflective, creative, and critical members of a variety of literacy communities.

Flexible Small-Group Instruction: What It Looks Like

Small, flexible groups are used to support individuals in their reading endeavors while providing a place where all voices can be heard and responded to as students come to terms with a book or piece of text. The five students in the following mixed-ability group were pulled together to do a short shared reading.

Deb begins the discussion by telling the group that she'd like to hear each of them read from *The Cay,* and, as they read, to let her hear what they are thinking, as she has demonstrated for them in a preliminary minilesson. Jennifer, as usual, eagerly volunteers to be first to read in the group. She's a very capable and avid reader. After she reads a sentence or two aloud, she stops to tell the group what she's thinking. In this case, she wonders aloud what "blackout curtains" are. She won't make a guess, but decides instead to keep reading. The answer to her question becomes clearer to her in the next few lines, and she stops to enlighten the group by saying, "Now I remember! They used blackout curtains to keep the enemy from seeing them at night. That way they wouldn't get bombed."

Deb asks Jennifer why she stopped when she first came to the term. Jennifer responds that she, of course, knew the words, but at first didn't get what blackout curtains meant. The group is then asked how they think Jennifer figured it out. Their answers were that

1. She had probably read about blackout curtains in another book.
2. She just kept reading, and the answer came to her.

Deb reinforces the students' findings by saying, "So, Jennifer first stopped because the term didn't make sense to her, and then she read on for more information. She also may have used information she'd learned in other books she'd read. Do the rest of you check to make sure you understand what you're reading as you read and then maybe reread or keep going to see if you can figure out something that gave you trouble?" The students nod.

"Who'd like to read next?" Deb asks.

After two other volunteers read and think aloud, Keith, a struggling reader, volunteers. He plods through the text and heaves a sigh of relief when he's finished. The other group members are quick to remind him that he forgot to tell them what he thought as he read. Keith is even quicker to mumble that all he had thought about was how much he hated reading aloud.

Deb says, "Let's try reading it together, and you stop all of us when you want to tell us what you're thinking about what we're all reading."

They read the next few sentences, and Keith says, "I think I wouldn't like getting sent away from my parents, even if my house was maybe gonna get bombed."

Here was a reader who was already responding to text but needed lots of support and practice in making his way through. Because supports such as reading aloud together are not uncommon activities in this classroom, because readers are encouraged to take risks, because mistakes and difficulties in reading are seen as opportunities for improvement rather than reasons for put-downs, and because kids' opinions are listened to and respected, Keith felt safe enough to express his views on the shared segment of text. The fact that his view became a springboard for further small-group discussion strengthened his and his classmates' belief that it's not only safe, but important, to share ideas.

Flexible Small-Group Instruction: Why It Looks That Way

Small groups consist of three to five students. Sometimes Deb will use small groups in conjunction with whole-group instruction, as we saw through the example of the *Sing Down the Moon* lesson. She created this short-term group on *The Cay,* on the other hand, specifically to give certain students in the group good models of how to think about reading as well as to give support in practicing thinking about reading. She chose other group members because they had demonstrated need for that kind of help. Throughout the year, Deb will use similar groupings to assess students' reading strengths and needs. The learning disabilities teacher also comes in during reading class to help with small-group support, and they both work with all of the groups.

Students in Deb's classroom work in small groups to:

- Discuss "chunks" of assigned or self-selected literature they read on their own or with partners.
- Work with Deb and one another on practicing reading strategies.
- Work with one another to create share-a-book products or explore an idea.

These groups vary in who they are, what they do, and how long they last according to the piece they're reading, their members' abilities to work together in a focused and supportive way, and where those members are in their development as readers. Throughout the year, however, Deb always sticks to two guidelines:

> Students apply a wide range of strategies to comprehend, interpret, evaluate, and appreciate texts. They draw on their prior experience, their interactions with other readers and writers, their knowledge of word meaning and other texts, their word identification strategies, and their understanding of textual features (e.g., sound-letter correspondence, sentence structure, context, graphics).

1. Groups meet simultaneously, but in different places in the classroom. In other words, with few exceptions, the whole class will be doing group work at the same time. This has worked best for Deb because nobody is disturbed during "quiet reading time."
2. Groups are *always focused and purposeful.* (As Deb says to her students, this is spelled "n-o g-o-o-f-i-n-g a-r-o-u-n-d.")

At the beginning of the year Deb arranges the small groups, making sure that each is mixed in terms of reading development, gender, and ethnicity. The class spends a great deal of time during the first quarter of school demonstrating and practicing working with a very few different reading group structures and activities in order to provide focused learning opportunities and develop students' abilities to work together. Thereafter, throughout the year, Deb varies the makeup and structure of the groups. Sometimes students group themselves according to book interest, sometimes Deb pulls a group together to focus on assessing or learning a certain reading strategy, and sometimes she puts a group together so they can listen and learn from one another's unique perspectives and experiences with text.

> Students develop an understanding of and respect for diversity in language use, patterns, and dialects across cultures, ethnic groups, geographic regions, and social roles.

These small groups can be role-specific or task-specific. An example of a role-specific group would be one in which each member is given a certain job to do in exploring a piece of text. As Harvey Daniels has illustrated, jobs can range from "text illuminator," who decides what piece of the day's reading will be read aloud, to "questioner," who writes two discussion questions, to "vocabulary expert," who finds three vocabulary words to discuss in the day's reading. An example of a task-specific group is one whose job is to work together to grapple with a piece of text to answer questions or write responses.

Deb and her class work hard at learning in small groups throughout the year, and she doesn't hesitate to rely on activities that have proven to be successful with certain groups. It is in these small groups that much of the "nitty-gritty" practicing of reading strategies is supported and evaluated. Deb touches base with each group daily, but she focuses most of her attention on one or two in particular. Here is how a typical reading "chunk" is handled using small groups at the beginning of the year:

- Short minilesson, focusing group
- Individual silent reading or reading of material with partner
- Small-group work to revisit the days' reading, handle student questions, share ideas, and focus on the minilesson.

As the year progresses, students become more comfortable and proficient with working in small groups, and they are given more responsibility and say in how the groups are structured.

Deb still struggles to answer the question, "What is it that successful readers do, and how do I provide experiences for learning and practicing these strategies for developing readers?" Knowing what to teach in large and small groups has been as big a question for her as how to teach. The lists of specific reading skills given in reading basals seemed unwieldy and disjointed to both her and her students. Kids who struggled with their reading in fifth grade had had plenty of work on those "skills" in earlier grades, yet they were still struggling. What is truly essential and important for them to learn and practice? Following is a list Deb uses that summarizes strategies, habits, and attitudes she believes are important to fifth graders' reading development. The list is a compilation and is not meant to be used as an isolated set of strategies taught out of context; rather, it serves to help focus Deb's instruction and assessment, as well as to help her remember the many strategies that proficient readers of any age orchestrate in order to construct meaning from print.

Strategies Worth Having and Teaching

- Planning to read, and previewing text (includes "draft" reading, skimming, and using pictures and textual clues)
- Predicting, checking correctness of predictions, and revising predictions (as a way to think through text material)
- Identifying information in a text (either the story line from a piece of fiction or main idea and supporting details from a piece of nonfiction); identifying literary elements is another form of this strategy
- Monitoring and self-correcting reading (asking, "Is this making sense to me? Could I explain this to a friend?")
- Responding to and reflecting on what's been read
- Generating questions about the text

- Figuring out unknown words (ways to do this are rereading, substituting a word, skipping a word, asking a friend, sounding a word out, reading on, or looking it up, all the while asking, "What meaning makes sense here? Does it look like a word I know? What sounds right?")
- Thinking about literary elements within a variety of literature types: these include character growth, mood, rising action/climax/falling action, foreshadowing and flashback, point of view, character study, commonalities of stories within a genre (e.g., what survival stories have in common), and author style.

Deb has three important reading goals for the kids in her classroom, goals that are of the utmost importance in reading development. These are:

- Reading fluency
- Positive and confident attitudes about books and reading
- Solid independent reading habits that create lifelong readers and learners (Deb believes strongly that aliteracy is as serious a problem as illiteracy).

The way that Deb teaches these strategies and elements is that she usually talks about them and demonstrates them during teacher read-aloud.

A Note on Assessment

One way of knowing whether students have successfully assimilated a strategy into their repertoires is to assess them. Deb tries to meet with each student once a week either in individual conferences or in small groups. She writes the student's name, the date, and strategies observed, using one sheet per student. In the conference, she'll ask about what the student is reading—usually, students are dying to tell her, even if they know Deb has read the material; she'll ask them to do a "read-aloud, think-aloud" on a piece of text, and she'll listen; or she'll ask a question pertaining to what they've read and what has been taught recently. For example:

> *Deb:* I noticed that you stumbled on the word *obstinate*. How did you figure that hard word out?
>
> *Student:* I kept going, and then I . . . I um . . . I went back. Then I sounded it out.
>
> *Deb:* Why would the character refer to her brother as "obstinate"?
>
> *Student:* Because he's a pain. He's stubborn!
>
> *Deb:* [smiles] Do you know someone who might be obstinate?
>
> *Student:* [laughs] Yeah. *My* brother!

During this time, Deb listens carefully to the student's responses and then takes her questions from them. She makes notes and records a plus, check, or minus to signal to herself how much further support a student might need with particular strategies or goals. None of this takes very long. It's important, of course, but most of the students' reading time is spent in reading and responding, as it should be. Most of Deb's time during reading is spent supporting students who need help, instructing and encouraging (sharing the job), and assessing.

Daily Independent Reading: What It Looks Like

Deb's program looks like this:

- Students read a self-selected book in class each day, and they respond in their literature logs to the section they've read. (Many students also choose to continue reading their books at home, which Deb encourages.)

- When students finish a book, they bring it and the "lit log" to Deb for a short conference. These conferences, though brief, are full of substance; they present another opportunity to pinpoint student progress and success, and they suggest strategies for individual use. More important, they provide students with a time for their voices to be heard by their teacher.

- Deb records the student's progress (noting the type of book read and reading behaviors and attitudes observed), and the student puts the title of the book on a list of completed books in his or her reading portfolio.

- The student signs up on the chalkboard for a book talk with a parent.

- When the parent arrives, he or she sets up shop in the hallway, checks the list on the chalkboard, and quietly takes a student, with his or her literature log and book, to the hall for a book chat.

- After the chat (no more than eight minutes), the parent writes a short, encouraging note to the student, places it in the classroom mailbox for distribution, and proceeds to work with the next student.

Here's how it works: As mentioned, time is provided each day for students' self-selected silent reading. Deb prefers to use the well-known term DEAR—drop everything and read—because the class never seems to be able to "get their reading time in" at the same time each day, although they do indeed work it in somewhere. Students may use the last five minutes of DEAR time writing responses into their literature logs. These logs do not have to be written in each day, but they must reflect students' thinking about literature as they read. Log entries must include the date, the book title and author, and the student's response to the text read. At the beginning of each year, as with the group work, Deb spends a great deal of time demonstrating what sorts of things to write in literature logs. This is also practiced and strengthened throughout the year.

The three following dialogues are typical of the short conferences Deb holds with students during DEAR time. When a student finishes reading a book, he or she brings it and his or her literature log to Deb's desk. Also, when Deb sees from her records that a student hasn't touched base with her in a while, she'll call that student to her desk to confer. Different needs are met within each of these conferences, depending upon where the student is in his or her reading process. Good teaching, is, after all, about what the student needs.

Dialogue: Deb and Linda

Linda has completed *The Ghost Next Door*, a self-selected book that she has read at school during silent

---

January 23, 1996 Roll of Thunder, Hear My Cry
Today I read about some kids walking to school. They donot like wearing their church clothes to school. I wouldn't like wearing my church clothes to school.

Jan. 29, 96
At school the teacher gives Cassie and Little Man books. Little Man threw down and stomped on the book because it called him a nigras he gets wiped. Now its getting exciting because its sad. Its sad because the people who sent the books only sent them because they were worn out. They give them the worn out ones because it was a African American school.

Feb. 5, 96
Today big ma has taken Cassie, Stacey, and T.J. to strawberry to sell eggs, milk, and other things. Now this book has really made me read.

reading time and at home. She has written dated responses in her literature log to sections of the book as she has read them, and she brings both the log and the book to Deb's desk for their conference. Deb reads through several of the responses, and they begin to talk. Linda is a very capable and reflective reader, but this time her log entries are few and lack the usual voice she uses in group discussions. The entries are mostly minisummaries of the book's events, without the usual level of insight and critical thinking Linda brings to her reading.

Deb: This book looks exciting, but I'm not sure it excited you.

Linda: It didn't.

Deb: You sound disappointed.

Linda: I am. I usually love Goosebump books. I've read a ton of 'em. This one just wasn't that good.

Deb: [glances at her records] Hmmm. You really have read a lot of Goosebump books! Why wasn't this one appealing to you? I noticed that you didn't have a lot to say about it in your lit log.

Linda: That's because there wasn't anything to say that I haven't said before. All of the books are starting to be sort of the same.

Deb: How's that?

Linda: You know.

Deb: Nope. I have to be honest with you. I've only read one R. L. Stine book. Fill me in.

Linda: Well, they start off pretty good and I want to keep reading. But after a while the problems start to seem alike, and the endings are . . . well, they're just the same, but different. Anyway, I don't believe the characters.

Deb: I'm not sure you're supposed to. Why do you suppose the book you were reading was written?

Linda: I think it was supposed to scare me, in a fun kind of way. It didn't, though. I hate to say it, but it was kind of boring.

Deb: Why did you stick with it?

Linda: I kept thinking it would get good.

Deb: I know what you mean. I've read books that way—I keep thinking that they'll get better. Lots of times they do. Sometimes they don't, though. Well, what about your next book?

Linda: I still want to read a scary book or maybe a mystery, but there aren't any good ones in the library.

Deb: Don't tell that to Ben.

Linda: What do you mean?

Deb: He loves mysteries, and he's raved about the last two books he's read. Remember his book boost last week?

Linda: Oh yeah! Mrs. Foertsch, can I go talk to Ben?

Deb: Sure. We'll touch base tomorrow, and you can let me know your plan.

Deb has listened carefully here to Linda's responses to her reading, and treated them with respect, while also suggesting how Linda might recapture her interest in reading.

Dialogue: Deb and Bobby

Deb notices from her records that Bobby hasn't requested a book conference with her yet this quarter. It has been two full weeks since she's touched base with him about his independent reading progress, and that is way too long. Bobby is a struggling, reluctant reader. He is well-behaved, but he often tries to "hide in the crowd" when it comes to his own reading. Although he needs a great deal of support in the actual reading of materials in small-group and whole-class work, Bobby often has genuine insights into the material shared. Deb calls Bobby to her desk. She glances at his log—his entries are sparse and sketchy, and he has switched books a number of times, completing only a very few independently so far this year.

Bobby: I haven't had much time to read this book.

Deb: It's been busy at home?

Bobby: Yeah. I've had soccer practice, and my dad's been out of town. I have a new dog . . .

Deb: Sounds like a busy family. But we do have DEAR time in school every day, so you do have some time to read. Maybe time is only part of the reason you're not reading as much as you'd like. It looks as if you've switched books quite a bit.

Bobby: Yeah. They were boring.

Deb: Why is that? You seem to enjoy the books we share together, and the books you've started don't look boring.

Bobby: No. It's just hard. I mean it takes me forever to even read a chapter. So I get bored and quit.

Deb: I see. What if you chose shorter books?

Bobby: No way I'm reading a baby book.

Deb: Not all short books are baby books, but OK. Is there a book that you've tried or that you've heard about that you'd just love to read?

Bobby: Well, I heard *Nightmare Mountain* was good.

Deb: That's an exciting one. Why don't you give it a spin? I bet you could find a friend who'd like to read this book with you. It might be fun to read the book together as book buddies. That way your friend could help you through any rough spots, and you could keep each other going throughout the story.

Bobby: Is it OK if I read with Trent? I think he's about done with his book.

Deb: Let's call him up here, and see if we can't get you two going.

Dialogue: Deb and Ben

Ben is a capable reader and a very creative thinker. Book talks with Ben tend to be rather one-sided throughout the year, with Ben doing lots of talking and Deb doing lots of listening and learning. He brings his book and literature log up for a conference. Deb reads through his entries on *Jurassic Park*, a book Ben's mother suggested to him.

Students apply a wide range of strategies to comprehend, interpret, evaluate, and appreciate texts. They draw on their prior experience, their interactions with other readers and writers, their knowledge of word meaning and other texts, their word identification strategies, and their understanding of textual features (e.g., sound-letter correspondence, sentence structure, context, graphics).

Deb: Jurassic Park! Have you seen the movie?

Ben: Yes, but the book was better.

Deb: How so?

Ben: Lots of ways. In the book, the ending left you more to think about, but the movie pretty much tied up all the loose ends. Also, the grandfather in the book was colder than in the movie. And did you know that it seems like the girl and the boy in the book had reversed personalities from the movie? In both the book and the movie, though, it seems like these pretty good intentions turn into a human disaster. Guess you've got to have something go wrong, though, or it would be a pretty boring story.

Deb: Whoa. Slow down. You've done a lot of thinking about this! Your lit log shows your excitement about the book, but let's say you take a few minutes to sit down and organize your ideas about how the book compares with the movie. Maybe do a Venn diagram.

Ben: OK. But I don't want to share it with the class, in case someone else is reading it at home.

Deb: OK. So share it with me. I've read the book and seen the movie too, and you've already got me thinking about how the two compare. I'd love to see your ideas on paper so I can keep up with them!

Ben: OK! I'll show it to you when I'm finished. I need some blank paper.

Deb: You know where it is. Help yourself.

Even the most skillful readers need to be pushed further to expand their thinking. Ben is wonderful at coming up with ideas, but Deb knows she has to help him focus and think through his conceptualizations more.

In each of these very different dialogues, student needs were noted, reading efforts were supported, and further explorations were encouraged. Conferences are as different as the students are. After each conference, Deb jots down student strengths and needs, as well as what she might do and watch for in order to encourage and support that student's reading efforts. She always keeps her list of strategies and goals in mind to help guide her written comments.

When students have completed a book and a teacher conference, they may sign up on the chalkboard for a book chat with the classroom's PALs (Partners Assisting Literacy). PALs are parents, grandparents, or other interested adults who volunteer throughout the year to come in to do book chats with Deb's students. These chats occur throughout the school day and week. Special times (music, P.E.) are not scheduled; instead, the volunteers come in once a week during a time convenient to them (but of course not during lunch or the class's special times). Deb doesn't send a letter to get volunteers to do book chats, but she does send out a general call for classroom volunteers at the beginning of the year, asking for field trip chaperons, etc. It's on this general call for help that she asks for book moms, dads, grandparents, guardians, foster parents, and the like.

Students participate as knowledgeable, reflective, creative, and critical members of a variety of literacy communities.

During the first week of school, she has a meeting with all those responsible for caring for her students outside the classroom, and she explains what book volunteers do and how it fits into her reading program. That's when the adults usually volunteer to help out.

After the PALs have volunteered, Deb gets together with them at a special meeting after school to go through how book chats work. After the volunteers know the routine, the book chats themselves are discussed, since this is usually of great concern. Some volunteers feel inadequate about what to say with the kids, and some are a little too eager to "teach those reading skills" or assess students' progress. Deb is careful to explain that the purpose of the chats is to lend an ear to the students' voices when they speak of a book they've been part of. The purpose of these book chats is to encourage further reading explorations, share viewpoints, dig deeper into the book. It's another way to give importance to students' literary experiences. (Yes, talking with other students does this too, but somehow, having a grownup's total attention, even for eight minutes, is especially valuable for kids.) Once the volunteers understand the purpose of the book chats, the group goes over some stimulating questions, listed below. Then Deb and a volunteer go through a mock book chat, using something Deb has recently read as a model. Volunteers are cautioned that they may have to "cut kids off" (gently, but firmly) from retelling the entire book with every detail. They are also cautioned not to run through the entire list of questions Deb provides; instead, she urges them to choose one or two from the list as a guide to discussing the book in more depth. The questions are simply given to provide some guidance, to serve as a "menu" to choose from in helping kids explore books.

The following questions and tips are written on a note card and thumbtacked to a bulletin board over a list of students who need to confer. Deb likes volunteers to start with question 1, since this is where kids really dig into their literature logs and books, and then choose one more question to follow up with.

After completing the conferences for the day, volunteers write brief, encouraging notes to the students. Kids love getting notes, and Deb sees them sharing them with friends. They've shared a few with her as well. A couple of samples: "Your book sounded so exciting! I'm glad you wouldn't tell me the ending. I'll check it out of the library tonight." "I agree

Questions to Use in Book Chats

1. Share a passage with me that: shows an emotion or a mood, uses interesting or beautiful language you don't totally understand, describes an important character, contains the climax of the book, reminds you of something in your own life. (Choose just one of these to explore with the student. Have him or her read the passage to you or summarize it if it's very long. Have the student explain/discuss.)

2. Does this book remind you of another you've read? How?

3. Would you read another book by this author? Why or why not?

4. What part of the book was the best, in your opinion? Why?

5. How did the main character in your book change from beginning to end?

6. What new facts did you learn from the book? What new insights or opinions do you have now?

7. What would you change about the book? Why?

8. What was especially challenging about this book?

9. What was especially effective about this book?

10. What was a problem in the book, and how was that problem resolved?

Tips

• Keep conferences positive and focused on students' sharing reflectively.

• Feel free to share your own insights, experiences, and ideas!

• Encourage further reading, please.

with you. I think you're ready to move on and read something more challenging. You might try . . ."

In class, before volunteers come for the first book chat of the year, Deb runs through the entire procedure with the students, and she holds a book conference with a student in front of the class. That way, students are prepared. During the rest of the year, the program runs pretty much automatically.

Some years, Deb has had seven or eight book volunteers, and some years she's only had one, but she's never had one who didn't love the experience. They can't believe the level of insight and emotion the kids bring to their reading and to the discussion. Sometimes, volunteers will go out and read a book because of a book chat they've had with a student. Usually, the volunteers use the questions Deb provides only at the beginning or if they get "stuck in a rut" throughout the year. The discussions occur naturally after the first few times with students. The kids, of course, love it, and it truly does encourage their independent reading and thinking.

Daily Independent Reading: Why It Looks That Way

This type of reading in Deb's classroom is much more than a just-sit-there-and-read experience. It gives Deb, as the teacher, a structured time to touch base with each student over a period of time, assess progress, and target instruction. Even more important, it gives students time to read what they want to read, practice and strengthen their reading powers, reflect upon what they've read, share what they've read, and receive the support they need for further reading explorations and reflections. The independent reading program plays a big part in building student habits of lifelong reading for the love of it.

Daily Teacher Read-Aloud: How It Looks

Each day, for at least fifteen minutes, Deb also reads aloud to the entire class. As Deb reads, she lends expression to the author's words. Deb practices her reading; never would she attempt to read a book out loud that she is not yet familiar with, and she stops throughout the read-aloud session to tell the class her thoughts about not only what's been read ("I think she'd better watch her step!"), but about how she's read it ("Did you hear how much better the poem sounded this time? Sometimes you just have to read it again to practice making the words flow"). Frequently, Deb solicits students' ideas about what the author might have meant in a certain passage, what might happen next, or what images or pictures the author's words are creating in their minds. Students regularly contribute their own ideas and questions, and spontaneous class cheers or sighs in response to the text are quite common. During read-aloud time, Deb asks that her students stay comfortable, listen quietly, participate in discussion, and follow along with their hearts and imaginations. This time is to be uninterrupted by drink or bathroom requests. Read-aloud time is a precious, important component in reading instruction. It is also one of the most pleasant times of the day.

Daily Teacher Read-Aloud: Why It Looks That Way

Teacher read-aloud time provides a natural setting for the demonstration of fluent, expressive reading. It is also an easy time for Deb and students to think about the text. Most important, however, it creates a tie that binds, giving them a common classroom language through shared literary experience. In choosing books for read-aloud, Deb aims for quality and variety. The books she reads often fit into a theme the class is studying, but just as often they don't. She reads from a variety of genres throughout the year so students can get a feel for different types of reading materials, and she varies the lengths of read-aloud pieces. Sometimes, she'll read entire novels to the class, section by section, day by day. Other times, she'll share picture books, letters, and, at least once a week, poetry. There is so much literature available that Deb feels strongly about her responsibility to help make sure her students listen to the best. She talks with both school and public librarians, colleagues, parents, and kids about what's new and good. She also reads many children's and young adult literature titles on her own throughout the school year and during the summer—especially during the summer! For her, it's one of the most pleasurable experiences of her professional life; the books move quickly and provide many good insights into the age group she teaches. In order to ensure variety while still maintaining quality and keeping the experience enjoyable for the students and herself, Deb has developed a list of questions to guide her literature choices:

Questions to Guide Literature Selections

1. Is it true? (In the case of nonfiction, are the facts accurate? In the case of fiction, does it demonstrate truths about life? Does the voice ring true?)
2. Is it important?
3. Is it "do-able" by fifth graders? (Can it be read independently or with support? Is it age-appropriate?)
4. Does the literature allow room for growth? (Does it accommodate or present differing perspectives? Does it inspire further reading and learning? Does it provide a good model for writing?)
5. Will it reach kids in the class? (Is it interesting and appealing to them? Can it be made interesting to them?)

The Poetree

As for variety, Deb feels the students' reading experience wouldn't be complete without poetry. On the back of a coat closet in the room is a bulletin board where a colorful tree, named "The Poetree," hangs. Clipped to this tree each week is an extra copy of a poem that has been distributed to the class for their mutual sharing and learning pleasure. Deb doesn't "do" a special poetry unit with the fifth graders. Instead, poetry is part of their weekly routine, a part of their classroom ritual.

A poem is copied and distributed to each student on Monday. Students read their personal copies as soon as they receive them; although the reading is supposed to be silent, in actuality that rarely happens. Usually, students whisper their responses: "This is a winner, Mrs. Foertsch!" or "I don't get the second stanza," or "Oh! I *get* it!" After the class has a few moments to read the poem through, either Deb or the student who brought it in reads it aloud for the class. Then they all read aloud together. Often, it takes another read-through to "get the beat" together or speak without stumbling over some of the words. Deb asks the kids to try the poem again on their own time and to think about the poem at home.

Throughout the school week, the class shares the poem aloud in class each day, frequently with small groups of volunteers reading the piece aloud and always ending with a whole-class rendition. This takes only a few moments, and on some days, that's all the class does. On other days, however, between the reading and the whole-class sharing, the class briefly discusses the poem, or Deb gives a minilesson using the poem as a basis for instruction.

Deb tries hard not to overdo the direct instruction, since she doesn't want to kill the joy of poetry by having students dissect every piece. However, the students seem to enjoy exploring the deeper meaning of a poem and looking for alliteration or pointing out patterns of rhyme. The minilessons also provide students with opportunities to examine the language of poetry more closely than they might on their own. Sometimes Deb will ask them to look at a phrase in a poem in order to help them think about their own writing. She might, for instance, ask, "How did the poet make this stanza especially descriptive? How might she have said it in a more boring way? Aren't we glad she cared enough to choose her ideas and words carefully?" Every year, Deb sees her students make the connection between reading and writing before her eyes, thanks to poetry.

Students read a wide range of literature from many periods in many genres to build an understanding of the many dimensions (e.g., philosophical, ethical, aesthetic) of human experience.

Frequently, the class will memorize the poem. Especially at the beginning of the year, Deb assigns the memorization and then supports students throughout the process. The class learns the poem together, aloud, a line or two at a time, always saying the first lines learned before attaching new lines. Practice is the key. They all discuss the "mental rehearsing" of a poem and relate it to mentally rehearsing a writing piece. They repeat the poem daily, and students who, at the beginning of the week, "can't do it," are frequently surprised that they know the poem by heart when Friday rolls around. On Friday, the class performs the poem. Most often, the performance is given in their own classroom with no outside audience, but occasionally the experience is shared with other classes. The poem is performed in ensembles—trios or quartets—and solos. Although it's true that the performances do at times get a bit repetitious, the students still look forward to "how Jill's going to do it," and they want to have an opportunity to share what they've learned. When the performances are finished, students file that week's poem in their individual poetry folders. Students love having a repertoire of poetry to choose from, and often poems from past weeks ("golden oldies") will be run through again.

Deb has found that she doesn't have to provide a poem for each week of the school year; after the first couple of weeks, students start bringing in poems on their own that they have found or that family members have suggested to them. The class especially enjoys finding poems (and sometimes speeches) that go along with themed units or the seasons of the year. Students bring in a mix of lengths and types of poems, always including lots of "fun" ones (written by Shel Silverstein or Jack Prelutsky, for example). The poems provide a rich fund of materials for performances and discussions throughout the year.

Occasionally, Deb will assess performances or activities based on mini-lessons. Students know in advance when Deb is assessing, and they frequently play a role in the assessment itself, whether it be deciding what's important to assess or participating in self- or group assessments.

Assessment and teaching about poetry are not the whole purpose of "doing the poems." The class "does" them because learning a poem builds students' confidence that they can indeed thoroughly know and understand a poem by Friday that looked impossible on Monday, because it strengthens the home-school connection when grandparents or primary caretakers help students learn, or because supper the night before might have been made richer because the student recited the poem for his or her family. Most important, poetry helps to create a common language for the class, giving all members of the community a shared background and frame of reference. Poetry "pops up" both inside and outside the classroom. On the playground, some kids will practice "their" poems with small groups of friends. The poetry becomes a kind of secret language or an inside joke that they're all in on.

The class's individual poetry folders are called "poetry pockets" in reference to the first poem used one year, "Keep a Poem in Your Pocket," by Beatrice Schenk de Regniers. There's a sign on the chalkboard under which homework responsibilities are listed. It reads, "Homework! Oh, Homework!"–a simple label from a poem by Jack Prelutsky that carries a deeper, amusing meaning for the students. And when the class takes a field trip to nearby woods, invariably someone will begin, "Whose woods these are I think I know," and that voice is joined by twenty-some others, "His house is in the village, though . . . "

Once students have begun, they can't be stopped–not that Deb would ever want to stop them! As one fifth grader put it, "Poems just come out of our heads and roll off our tongues." *That's* why they "do" poetry.

Keep a Poem in Your Pocket

Keep a poem in your pocket
and a picture in your head
and you'll never feel lonely
at night when you're in bed.

The little poem will sing to you
the little picture bring to you
a dozen dreams to dance to you
at night when you're in bed.

So—
Keep a picture in your pocket
and a poem in your head
and you'll never feel lonely
at night when you're in bed.

Beatrice Schenk de Regniers

Daily Book Boosts and Book Sharing: What They Look Like

Each day at the end of their "official" reading time, Deb has students give "book boosts," one-minute raves about books they've read. Two students per day are assigned to give the boosts, and they're required to follow four rules when doing so:

1. They have to have read the book.
2. They have to really love the book. Deb often says, "It's a book boost, not a book bust!"
3. They have to keep the boost to one minute.
4. They mustn't give away the book's ending.

Deb chooses students in the order in which they're seated in their circle of desks so that they know when their turn is coming. Book boosts are required activities, and time is spent during the beginning of the year demonstrating and practicing them. Although Deb keeps track of the boosts, she doesn't usually assess them, because she hasn't needed to. The students' eagerness to share their enthusiasm for the books they speak about illustrate that the activity's goals have been met. Nor does she require any written preparation. However, the class does keep a file of favorite fifth-grade books that students add to

Students adjust their use of spoken, written, and visual language (e.g., conventions, style, vocabulary) to communicate effectively with a variety of audiences and for different purposes.

throughout the year. It's another opportunity for everyone to learn about new titles, and for Deb to get a realistic perspective on the kinds of material her students respond to.

Of course, book boosts aren't the only way books are shared in the classroom. Frequently, when groups or individual students have completed books they have loved, they are eager to share their excitement with others, both inside and outside the classroom. Students themselves decide how best to share their books— whether it be through a book chat, a letter, a video, a poster, or another form—and will either design and execute these book-sharing projects on their own time or in small groups.

Daily Book Boosts and Book Sharing: Why They Look That Way

The book boosts and the class's Good Book File are easy ways to suggest a multitude of titles to students, and they act as a way for students to have something to think about as they read. They provide students with the opportunity to celebrate successful milestones in their literacy explorations by sharing books and ideas with other students, who, in turn, are encouraged in their own explorations. Books become personalized as individual student voices exclaim a book's wonders. It's exciting to see kids seeking out Joy's book for their own reading pleasure. It's fun to watch students wait in line because they "want to be put on the waiting list for Rashad's book." It's inspiring to see Jaime's opinion being sought after because "he can always pick a good one." It's important that students listen to and value one another as readers and fellow explorers.

Book Clubs "Just for Fun": What They Look Like

Book clubs are an important part of reading in Deb's classroom. The procedure is loose:

1. Students decide what book to read and with whom they want to read it.
2. Students read the book, discussing it along the way.
3. Students share the book with others or sign up and meet with Deb for a "lunch bunch" conference.

The only rule Deb has for book clubs is, "No 'ugliness' about who's reading what with whom." She makes it clear that there is no room for comments like "Sam's not allowed in our book club" in their classroom community. Because the teacher won't allow it, because students consider book clubs to be very important, and because all members of the community work hard to support one another's reading efforts, students rarely break the "no ugliness" rule. They enjoy the choice in books, the choice in how to respond to the books, and the choice in whom they get to read with.

"Lunch bunch" conferences are informal chats about a book club's completed selection. A book club requests a lunch bunch time, and Deb meets with the students in the classroom to talk about the book as they eat. These sessions are held at noon recess and lunchtime to discuss a book just for pleasure, and Deb doesn't evaluate the content of the conversation. Mostly, she simply listens, joins in, and enjoys. Students choose their own groups for these meetings, and most of the students participate at times throughout the year. Sadly, however, there are always a few kids who choose not to participate at all. (A few don't like giving up their noon recess or lunch period, and Deb doesn't require that they do so.) Lunch bunch is an "extra" to encourage students' independent reading and chatting about books. It helps that most times Deb brings brownies to share, of course!

For example: three girls—Angela, Janie, and Su Ling, of varying reading abilities—had decided to read Lois Lowry's *Number the Stars* together. They met every other day or so to briefly discuss what they'd read and to map out how much to read next. This reading-together experience was their own idea and was new to them. Their predictions of what would happen next in the book came naturally in the discussions Deb listened in on, and she was especially pleased that the group was sustaining the mighty efforts of Angela, who had to work hard to keep pace with the others. The way the three friends supported one another during their reading of the book was a tribute to their appreciation of their differences and to their friendship. ("Does everyone think we can do this much by Tuesday? I know we're dying to know if Ellen makes it, but we don't want to go too fast.") Deb knew first thing in the morning when the girls had completed their reading the evening before because she was greeted at the door with, "In for lunch bunch tomorrow!" and, "Mrs. Foertsch, it was so good!" After attendance, they bounded to her desk to make their official appointment. The next noontime in their classroom, after their classmates had gone to the lunchroom and the girls had commented on their food ("My mom makes me eat this but I hate it," "Do you always have that for lunch, Mrs. Foertsch?"), the discussion began in earnest.

> *Deb:* Well, I can tell that you enjoyed the book and had fun reading it together. It's a good story!
>
> *Janie:* It's an important story!
>
> *Deb:* I agree. I've read the book too. So, tell me why it's important.
>
> *Janie:* It's about a true event, the Holocaust, and it *is* true that many Dutch people helped Jews to escape or hide from the Nazis. I know because my parents told me. I learned about it at home.
>
> *Su Ling:* Yeah, but the book isn't true. The book is fiction. Lois Lowry made it up, even though part of it's true, like what happened to the

Students participate as knowledgeable, reflective, creative, and critical members of a variety of literacy communities.

Jews in the Holocaust. The characters aren't real, but they sure seemed real.

[Giggles]

Deb: What's so funny?

Janie: We decided that we're like the girls in the book! I'm Jewish and Angela and Su Ling are Christian. Our parents are friends like Annemarie's and Ellen's parents. And one of us has an annoying little sister!

[More giggles, accompanied by nods and knowing looks]

Angela: Plus we're good friends, and we would help each other like they did in the book. We would pretend that we're sisters like Ellen and Annemarie did and think of a way to get out.

Deb: That took a lot of courage on everyone's part.

Su Ling: They were all very brave, except the Nazis.

[Nods]

Janie: I liked the part where Annemarie got stopped by the Nazis on her way to give her uncle the basket.

Angela: Me, too. I couldn't figure out about the handkerchief, though.

Janie and Su Ling: Neither could we.

Deb: So, do you get it now?

Su Ling: Of course. It told in the book.

Angela: Yeah. We just kept reading. The scent on the handkerchief made the dogs unable to sniff out the people hiding.

Deb: So you understood that if you just kept reading in this case, the author would help you figure out what was happening. That's a good strategy. Any other challenges in reading the book?

Angela: Some of those names! I got help from my mom on them.

Su Ling: Not me. I just sounded them out as best I could and kept reading. There weren't too many of them, so I didn't let it get to me.

Janie: But what did get to me was that I didn't think we'd ever find out more about how Annemarie's older sister died. But we did. And it was kind of sad that her fiancée died too.

Deb: Why do you think Lois Lowry put those sad parts in?

Su Ling: Because that's life, Mrs. Foertsch! She wanted to make it real and not make it sicky-sweet. That's one of the reasons I liked this book so much.

Deb: Not all sicky-sweet?

[Nods around the table]

Deb: If you had to give a one-word answer to what *Number the Stars* was about, what word would you give?

Janie: Holocaust.

Su Ling: Yeah. War or escape.

Angela: Friends. Now it's your turn, Mrs. Foertsch.

Deb: I'd say, friends growing up, showing tremendous courage, and being there for each other to get through the horrors of the Holocaust.

Girls: No fair! You said to use one word!

In this lunch bunch, the book club participants shared various reading strategies, related their own life experiences to the book, shared lunch, and strengthened friendships. Not bad for half an hour.

Book Clubs "Just for Fun": Why They Look That Way

In this classroom, "just for fun" book clubs are student-organized and student-driven. These book clubs happen outside of school, at recess, and at times during small-group reading. Toward the beginning of the year, students are shown where the literature sets are kept, and they're invited to share a book with some friends. However, no one is allowed to borrow a literature set book without Deb's permission (this is unlike the classroom library corner, where books come and go as the students please). That way, Deb can use the literature sets to promote book clubs to "friends-to-be" (she is often heard saying such things as, "Did you know Sarah and Jill have chosen that book too?"), without actually keeping track or control of who's in what club, which would defeat the purpose of student initiative. This is, after all, "just for fun." Of course, students are not limited to using only the literature sets in the classroom; frequently, book clubs will spring up around multiple copies in the school library during the once-a-week "official" library checkout time. Kids have even been heard to argue, "It must be a good book. They wouldn't have bought four copies of it if it was boring and nobody read it."

Book clubs are opportunities for students to choose what they read, when they read, where they read, how they read, and with whom they read. The key concept here is choice. Kids value it. Another key concept is to keep the clubs special. Deb does that by requiring students to ask permission to read the literature sets, which automatically makes the books coveted. At times, she will also invite book clubs to meet at small-group time during reading, which is a special occasion that gives the students a good deal of freedom and responsibility in running their own groups.

In order to carry out book clubs successfully, students must work together to negotiate places and times to meet, along with the pacing and discussion of the books. They take on responsibility for their own literacy learning. They learn to value one another as readers and learners.

Stepping Back, Looking In

Reading instruction in this classroom is grounded in Deb's own journey. Along the way, she's gathered beliefs about how kids best learn and how she best teaches, and these beliefs, together with what she believes is important to learn, form the base from which she teaches. Instruction is viewed as explo-

Students use spoken, written, and visual language to accomplish their own purposes (e.g., for learning, enjoyment, persuasion, and the exchange of information).

ration, opportunities are many, and student learners are challenged, enticed, and valued. Deb's journey continues with further questions to explore and consider:

- The inclusion of students with special needs into the "regular" classroom presents a number of new challenges. Questions here are as varied as the students served: What is the best way to share teaching responsibilities with special education teachers who now come into the classroom to meet the needs of all students? How do teachers work together to accommodate their different philosophies, experience levels, schedules, and teaching styles so that students come out on top? How should instruction be modified to meet all students' needs? Where will the time to plan for these accommodations come from? And, more important, how can teachers make literature truly accessible to all students?

- Deb knows that everyone in the class works hard to demonstrate the value of each student's voice in large and small groups. Yet she also knows that when small groups are meeting, even though students are "doing what they're supposed to do," her presence at these groups is overly valued. Not that students shouldn't value her presence. She's happy to be counted as an important person in their literature journeys. But it's difficult to convince students that their small groups and literature talks count even when she's working with another group, that talking about books at recess counts, that their own ideas count. How can she get this across?

Then there's always the assessment quandary. Deb received a phone call recently from a caring mother, a polite but concerned mother. Her son hadn't been accepted into the school's gifted program for the following year. Not all of his achievement scores were in the ninety-fifth percentile or above. Yet she knows that her son is a gifted learner and thinker and writer and reader. She, too, appreciates his wonderful sense of humor and curiosity, and his persistence in pursuing and manipulating ideas. But test scores had deprived him of an opportunity. Not fair. Maybe, the mother suggested, he'd needed more practice with the multiple-choice test format before taking the achievement tests. Maybe. Does Deb teach only what she believes is important? What she's learned is important? Or does she "give in" and give over more precious instruction time to the teaching of "test-taking skills" in order to please parents and better "prepare" students for the too-powerful tests? Is there a happy medium to be found?

Questions such as these for her to consider will always come up. And Deb will continue to search and explore. She has learned to enjoy this very important part of the process. It makes her an even better teacher.

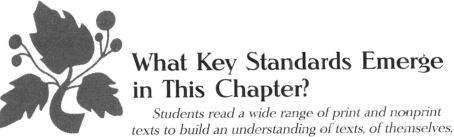

What Key Standards Emerge in This Chapter?

Students read a wide range of print and nonprint texts to build an understanding of texts, of themselves, and of the cultures of the United States and the world; to acquire new information; to respond to the needs and demands of society and the workplace; and for personal fulfillment. Among these texts are fiction and nonfiction, classic and contemporary works.

Deb helps the students connect their reading of *Sing Down the Moon* with what they know in their lives, both by discussing the text with the students as a whole group, asking the students to discuss Bright Morning's qualities in small groups, and having individuals write their responses down for themselves. She encourages the students to understand the conventions of the text by asking them to find illustrations of Bright Morning's characteristics in the book itself, and then she takes the process a step further by asking them to think of how those characteristics apply in their own lives. In this way, Native American culture becomes more meaningful; rather than studying discrete, abstract concepts, the students learn to understand the commonalities involved with all people, and the importance of respecting different cultures. The book talks, parent volunteer book chats, and "lunch bunch" meetings that Deb has with the students also reinforce talk as a way of understanding text.

Students read a wide range of literature from many periods in many genres to build an understanding of the many dimensions (e.g., philosophical, ethical, aesthetic) of human experience.

Again, the students' connecting the qualities they see in Bright Morning with the qualities they value in themselves helps them gain a deeper understanding of what it means to be human. In addition to fiction, students read poetry (as illustrated by "The Poetree"), science fiction, and historical fiction from various cultures and times. Books such as *Jurassic Park, Number the Stars,* and *The Cay* are all from perspectives and times different from students' lives and allow students to experience other worlds in a rich and fulfilling way.

Students apply a wide range of strategies to comprehend, interpret, evaluate, and appreciate texts. They draw on their prior experience, their interactions with other readers and writers, their knowledge of word meaning and other texts, their word identification strategies, and their understanding of textual features (e.g., sound-letter correspondence, sentence structure, context, graphics).

In their whole-group discussions, students think out loud about what strategies they use in their reading. For example, when the term "blackout curtains" gives Jennifer trouble she pauses but then reads on to try to "get" its meaning from the context, also drawing on earlier reading that might have introduced her to the term. Both strategies are reinforced for students by Deb's asking students to think aloud as they read and compare strategies. Students also ask questions of themselves and their reading that they might not otherwise. The example of finding characteristics inherent in Bright Morning help students understand literary conventions such as an author's creation of character.

Students participate as knowledgeable, reflective, creative, and critical members of a variety of literacy communities.

The dynamic interaction encouraged in Deb's classroom helps the students become active participants, and because they have the room to do so, they show themselves to be insightful, eager, and reflective learners.

References and Resources for Further Reading

Calkins, L. (1987). *The art of teaching writing*. Portsmouth, NH: Heinemann.

Crichton, M. (1990). *Jurassic park*. New York: Knopf.

Daniels, H. (1994). *Literature circles: Voice and choice in the student-centered classroom*. York, ME: Stenhouse.

de Regniers, B. S. (1958). *Something special*. New York: Harcourt, Brace.

Frank, M. (1995). *If you're trying to teach kids how to write . . . you've gotta have this book!* Nashville, TN: Incentive.

Graves, D. (1983). *Writing: Teachers and children at work*. Portsmouth, NH: Heinemann.

Interactive classroom, The. (1995). El Cajon, CA: Interaction Publishers.

Kehret, P. (1989). *Nightmare mountain*. Illus. E. McKeating. New York: Dutton Children's Books.

Lowry, L. (1989). *Number the stars*. Boston: Houghton Mifflin.

O'Dell, S. (1970). *Sing down the moon*. Boston: Houghton Mifflin.

Prelutsky, J. (1984). *The new kid on the block*. Illus. J. Stevenson. New York: Greenwillow.

Primary Voices K–6. National Council of Teachers of English.

Routman, R. (1991). *Invitations: Changing as teachers and learners, K–12*. Portsmouth, NH: Heinemann.

Stine, R. L. (1993). *Goosebumps: The ghost next door*. New York: Scholastic.

Taylor, M. D. (1976). *Roll of thunder, hear my cry*. Illus. J. Pinkney. New York: Dial Books for Young Readers.

Taylor, T. (1969). *The cay*. Garden City, NY: Doubleday.

Wayne–Finger Lakes BOCES, Department of Staff Development. (n.d.). *Frameworks: A whole language staff development program for grades K–8*. Stanley, NY: Author.

CHAPTER TWO

FREEDOM TO WRITE

The First Discussion

A group of twenty-two third graders—squirming, giggling, showing gaps in their mouths where baby teeth used to be—sit with Jan Ewing on a comfortable blue braided rug in one corner of the room. All are involved in discussing their new schedule and writers' workshop, the block of time in which their daily writing takes place. Jan has just finished talking about being self-directed and independent—two big words expressing even bigger concepts for these mostly eight- and nine-year-old children. No longer will they be assigned topics and styles of writing.

"You're not *ever* going to tell us what to write about?" Ajay, a quiet boy with serious eyes, asks. "Never ever?"

Jan smiles. "No, I won't tell you what to write. Your writing is exactly that. *Your* writing. It is your responsibility to write, and you will have the freedom to choose what to write about."

"Wait a minute," says Minh-ha, a girl who wriggles with pent-up energy. "We get to spend time every day writing and you won't give us the ideas or titles?"

"That's right," Jan says.

"Does that mean we can write about anything we want?" Eric asks.

"That's pretty much what it means," Jan says. "Let's talk some more about that."

And so begins the first of what are to be many discussions about writing, ideas, thoughts, expression, and writers' workshop.

Based on her previous experiences with students and writing, knowledge she has gained from reading a great deal, and on her own reaction to different situations as a writer, Jan has decided to incorporate writing process into the curriculum. To many, writing process looks like the following progression of steps: prewriting (also known as freewriting), drafting, revising, clarifying, and editing. But these "steps" are by no means linear or sequential—they are part of a very fluid process, and might be thought of instead as stages. Some students, for instance, might skip the prewriting stage and move to drafting, then skip clarifying because the piece is clear enough already. Jan talks about these stages with the class, asking for examples from students of what each means to them individually. They talk about idea-gathering strategies and discuss the value of having time to think.

Students employ a wide range of strategies as they write and use different writing process elements appropriately to communicate with different audiences for a variety of purposes.

Right now they focus on prewriting/freewriting—a part of the process that emphasizes spontaneity and getting ideas and thoughts down on paper without worrying about coherence. The goal of freewriting is to capture and enhance the creative flow that accompanies higher-order thinking. Mechanics will come later, once the students know what they want to say in their pieces and can connect clear grammar and correctly spelled words with the messages they want to communicate. In that way, grammar, spelling, and vocabulary mean something in context to the writers, and they are much more likely to remember learned concepts and apply them in meaningful ways throughout their lives. Right now it is important for the students to feel engaged with their writing, to understand how exciting it can be to share thoughts and feelings that are important to them. An existing writers' workshop curriculum that encouraged individual writing already existed, but Jan knew that it didn't go far enough to develop truly independent writers. She also knew that if she wanted the outcome to be purposeful writing with ever-increasing writing skills, she and the class would have to create a structure to hold their writing experiences together.

Students apply knowledge of language structure, language conventions (e.g., spelling and punctuation), media techniques, figurative language, and genre to create, critique, and discuss print and nonprint texts.

In order for the children to make as smooth a transition as possible, the structure would be simple: each student would be expected to write and to make use of the writing process each day. Over time, Jan knew the students would define their own purposes and develop their unique styles of writing. For now, she hoped that writers' workshop would be a time for them to express themselves. The class talks in detail about how they'll have time each day to write without interruptions, without rushing, and without being told what and how to write. The students will choose topics that are of interest to them. They do not have to have each topic approved, but as a class they discuss how all topics and the language in their writing need to be school-appropriate. All agree that it is necessary to take the responsibility of authorship seriously and to communicate in the very best possible way.

Students use spoken, written, and visual language to accomplish their own purposes (e.g., for learning, enjoyment, persuasion, and the exchange of information).

Over the next few weeks, decisions are made daily about where and when to work on pieces. The students work independently, with partners, or in small groups. From day to day, the configuration of writers changes. Children choose to work on realistic fiction, fantasy, science fiction, sports stories, and mysteries. Some children write factual accounts of events and time periods. The common foundation is that each day everyone is involved with the writing process.

During writers' workshop students sit on the floor, the rug, at their desks—anywhere they can find a comfortable and secure place to work. They sit with friends or alone, in a variety of positions. Each child spends time writing, sharing writing, reading their writing silently or out loud to a partner, listening to or reading a friend's writing, talking and thinking about writing. The message is clear—everyone in the class is a writer, and writing is important.

Writers' Workshop Folders

Although Jan could see how excited the children were about writers' workshop, she was still surprised at how important their writing folders were to them.

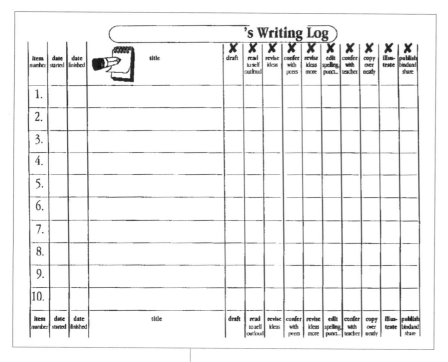

item number	date started	date finished	title	draft	read to self outloud	revise ideas	confer with peers	revise ideas more	edit spelling punct...	confer with teacher	copy over neatly	illus- trate	publish bindand share
			's Writing Log	X	X	X	X	X	X	X	X	X	X
1.													
2.													
3.													
4.													
5.													
6.													
7.													
8.													
9.													
10.													
item number	date started	date finished	title	draft	read to self outloud	revise ideas	confer with peers	revise ideas more	edit spelling punct...	confer with teacher	copy over neatly	illus- trate	publish bindand share

She gave each student a two-pocket folder, a legal pad, and a pad of stick-on notes. After the students decorated and personalized the folders, Jan showed the class a basket on a counter—this would be where the folders were kept (it didn't take long for some students to have two folders—one for works in progress, the other for finished pieces or pieces no longer of interest). Not only do the students take extra care of their own written work, but Jan is continually surprised by the special attention they give to preserving the work of others.

So that the students can be reflective and thoughtful about their work, Jan provides them with a check-off sheet to keep track of progress with individual pieces. The students gain a sense of accomplishment from listing their stories, and they learn more about writing by using many of the options available for creating a real working piece of writing.

Jan knew that for writing to be valued, she would need to demonstrate respect for student pieces. Therefore, she does not read any story without an author's permission, and neither does anyone else. She does not share an individual's work with the rest of the class without permission either. The freedom to write has to be supported by respect for the work the children create.

Continuing Discussions

Jan and the students often have large- and small-group discussions about writing. These occur at various times throughout writers' workshop, and are initiated by the students, by Jan, or by both. Sometimes problems surface that need to be resolved, and sometimes there are recurring difficulties that need to be explored, such as copying others' ideas, making negative comments about writing, having difficulty collaborating with others, and being unclear about having responsibility as an author. Jan acts as a discussion facilitator, enabling the students to express their opinions, and the students offer solutions and alternatives to problems. The class works together; when a problem is resolved the solution has to be agreeable to everyone. At the same time, when minor issues are encountered, individuals are expected to come up with their own resolutions in order to develop confidence and independence in their thinking.

The children are encouraged to share their ideas about how they envision their writers' workshop. They talk about how they write, what they write, and what they plan to write. They discuss their individual working styles, and whether they enjoy working alone or with friends. They talk about their feelings when they share their work, and they discuss what makes it difficult or easy to do so. Some students speak about working in the same place every day; others

Students participate as knowledgeable, reflective, creative, and critical members of a variety of literacy communities.

talk about moving around the classroom and trying out new spots. They share reactions to one another's writing. Continual class discussions help Jan and the students focus on the importance of their daily writing and help them become more and more familiar with the writing process in ways that make sense to them based on their individual experiences. Because of that, the class has decided to add two of their own steps—direction and sharing. Direction is a time for discussion midway through the process, when alternatives to pieces can be explored. The addition of the sharing step demonstrates the students' desire to have a piece read and discussed with an adult. Jan is happy to see the class moving from developing ideas to completing written work.

Students employ a wide range of strategies as they write and use different writing process elements appropriately to communicate with different audiences for a variety of purposes.

Conferences

In order to help her remember where students have started from and to document their progress throughout the school year, Jan talks with each writer at least once a week in a formal and documented way. She chose not to set up a schedule but instead circulates around the room to talk with individuals. She uses a class list to record the authors she visits and saves specific notes on each author's work in a folder. At the beginning of the year, her role was that of an encourager and questioner. She would listen to and ask about the work that was presently being written, and she would question the direction and the future of a piece. The children are open about discussing their work, their attitudes about writing, and what Jan can do to help their efforts. All are capable of discussing specific details, and they are also able to compare their pieces as their work increases in volume. Jan's role is to track and note the level of the author's involvement, to be observant about any change in attitude, and to note and work through with students any difficulties that might cause frustration or discontent with writing.

Conferring by moving around the room and going to the student enables Jan to be less invasive. She can sit and observe until an author reaches a good stopping point. Together, they discuss all aspects of the writing process, which includes Jan in the discussion but lessens the temptation for either her or the student to think of her as an evaluator or expert. The child's thoughts and opinions about a piece are always emphasized; these are truly conference conversations. As the students' confidence in their writing increased, Jan found herself listening and supporting them more and more. Her notes from the conferences include the titles of works, the projected future writing focus (to edit, illustrate, publish, or begin with another idea), as well as comments about the most striking features of the author's writing.

Parent Volunteers

Jan knew that in order to best meet the needs of the children, she would need to enlist the help of parents, who volunteered to come to writers' workshop daily to edit, give direction, and share student pieces. Prior to class involvement, Jan invited the parents to attend a meeting, where she outlined their roles as encouragers, listeners, and editors. Their job is to be a positive part of the writing process. Each parent volunteer is given a folder containing information about writing, the writers' workshop format, definitions of the stages

of the writing process, and blank paper for notes or concerns. It is Jan's responsibility to be available to help parent volunteers feel confident and able to be a meaningful part of the process for the students. She continually observes and offers help when needed. She also makes it a point to talk briefly with parents as often as possible and expresses appreciation for the time they devote to helping the students.

In order to make best use of the time available, the students have agreed to sign up on the chalkboard for whatever they need during writers' workshop. The list has columns for publishing, editing, sharing, and direction, and students are free to sign up at any point.

Revising

Revising is often confused with editing, but it's actually a much different part of the writing process. If a student isn't sure where to go with a piece or feels a piece is almost finished, he or she gives it to a parent and asks for feedback. At this point, the parent responds by asking the writer questions, helping to point out what works well in the piece as well as where story elaboration or modification might be needed. The students enjoy hearing detailed verbal feedback about their writing and are eager to receive comments about their work, whether it is finished or in progress. Often, the authors share their stories again and again with different audiences. Some enjoy reading pieces aloud; others prefer that their work be read silently.

If a writer is stuck and has not found the time allowed for independent thought to be helpful, he or she can seek out direction, a part of the revision process that Jan and the students came up with themselves. The focus of direction is to make a decision about what to do and to articulate that decision. Parents support the brainstorming that follows by helping the students list possibilities and offering encouragement for different ideas to be tried out. If one idea doesn't work, the parent and the writer together explore others. Direction is usually a discussion that ends with a decision about what to do next. The student then works more on the piece until he or she feels it is finished conceptually, and then editing begins.

Editing

A basic editing routine is followed. The student/author brings his or her work, a marker, and stick-on notes to a parent volunteer during an editing session. The writing ideas need to come from the student/author, but the parent is expected to offer suggestions to enrich the writing being discussed. Editing consists of a specific routine with these steps:

- The author reads the piece aloud to give the parent editor a general understanding of it.
- The child and parent editor go over the piece together, rereading and editing for mechanical errors.

Students adjust their use of spoken, written, and visual language (e.g., conventions, style, vocabulary) to communicate effectively with a variety of audiences and for different purposes.

- Any misspelled words are put on stick-on notes to be used later as spelling words, and spelling is corrected within the piece.
- The child then tells the parent editor what he or she is planning to do next with the work. This includes stopping and moving to other pieces to work on, continuing with a final draft, or spending time illustrating or sharing.

The students are involved in the editing process by reading their work aloud to the parent editor and then by following along as the editor edits for punctuation, capitalization, spelling, and paragraphing.

During one of their class discussions, the students and Jan came to an agreement that editing, among other things, meant that the story will not be changed totally. They also agreed that ownership of writing is theirs. and that in the end they have to agree with any changes or modifications made. If an author does not like certain changes, it is time to work with another parent editor or with Jan in order to regain interest and control of the work. A student can also call an editing conference, in which Jan talks with the student and the parent editor about the editing process for a particular piece. Together. they will come to a resolution that is satisfactory to all three.

Jan is intrigued that most of the students know exactly what they want to do with their work after editing; few of them need help in getting direction. The parent volunteers enable the writers to be on task and move with direction and purpose on a daily basis—on the days when there is no parent support available, much less is accomplished. Fortunately, two or three parents are usually in the classroom to help.

Publishing

The class as a whole has explored ways in which to publish their work; many options and materials are available, and parent volunteers oversee the process by helping the students as much or as little as needed. The most popular way to publish a piece is to create a book using cereal boxes and contact paper, collected by Jan and the students, and enough books have been made in a wide variety of sizes, colors, and patterns for the class to create its own library. Everyone spends time reading and rereading the collection—by the end of the first year, there were over three hundred books to choose from. At the end of each school year, authors take their work home with them.

Writers at Work

Each and every one of the students in Jan's class approaches writers' workshop as an adventure. It is a time to discover, to express ideas, and to find contentment as authors. The profiles of the following five writers are an attempt to offer a picture of what the development of independent, confident, capable writers looks like.

Anna

From the first writers' workshop, Anna was motivated, enthusiastic, and eager to write. Her ideas were endless, and her creativity was evident in each piece. Anna's excitement about writing was contagious. She was a prolific writer and wrote over fifty stories during the year. Anna's most popular works were her series of books—*The Field Trip, The Field Trip II (Lost in the Air), The Field*

The Field Trip

By Anna Birnberg
Pictures By
Emelia Lesser

Trip III, *The Field Trip IV (Lost in Vegas), The Field Trip V,* and *The Field Trip VI (The Very Last Field Trip)*. The whole class was included as the main characters for the series. Anna's humor and wit were inspirational and encouraged other students to use humor in their pieces. Anna used a routine aspect of school—field trips—and imaginatively enriched the subject for herself and others. Her technique gave many of the other children ideas of how to combine their experiences with fantasy. Anna's total involvement in writing, her extensive use of the writing process, and her ability to publish her own books were motivating and encouraging to everyone.

Victor

Using his own life experiences as the subjects, Victor wrote many stories. The characters were often Victor's family, friends, or pets, and the plots were enhanced bits of reality with surprises and twists. Victor's positive attitude about writing and writers' workshop permeated his use of every part of the writing process. Victor especially enjoyed sharing stories with friends, and reciprocated by being an excellent listener, commenting in meaningful ways about friends' stories. Illustrations were an important part of his published works, and Victor took great pride in his written accomplishments as well.

Danny

At first, Danny seemed to want to be given ideas, topics, or the beginning of a story to write (this often occurs, and it's important to offer guidance to help provide scaffolding for the writer's eventual independence). He wasn't sure what to write about and benefited from encouragement and discussions about the value of thought time. Danny also enjoyed being an idea gatherer; he read stories, looked through magazines, and read and listened to his friends' work. Then Danny began to develop ideas. His first story, a picture book, was greatly enhanced by his artistic capabilities. Once Danny began to share his ideas, he found that he liked his classmates' reactions. First, he developed a series of stories about stupid animals. Later in the year, he was the first in the class to write short mysteries that required the reader to come up with solutions (the answer would be written on the following page). This idea became extremely popular, and many kinds of mysteries were written by other students after Danny published his.

Billy

Billy spent most of writers' workshop in the company of friends. He especially enjoyed working with his peers and would use them as monitors of his thoughts, his spelling, and the sequencing of his stories. Sports were his favorite topic, and the Chicago Bulls, featuring Michael Jordan and Benny the Bull (the Bulls' mascot), were usually the focus of his pieces. Billy's stories typically revolved around a game or a season of games; he was able to write thoughtfully about his experiences and demonstrated a writer's sense of understanding the creative process.

LaWanda

LaWanda could be found every day in the corner created by the hall and the classroom, singing as she wrote. Everyone knew where LaWanda spent writers' workshop; she was a true writer, in the sense that she so enjoyed writing that she had more writing than she could publish and had to be selective about what worked best. She loved expressing her thoughts on paper—her focus was not first of all on the final product, or on just completing a piece, but on the process of writing and thinking about writing itself. She enjoyed sharing her stories and reading them aloud, and she would also listen carefully while friends read their stories to her. LaWanda always had a positive comment to give and her reaction to her own writing was as consistently reflective and thoughtful.

Jan's Role as Teacher

Jan is always quick to say that the children's devoted involvement defines her role as a teacher. Their focus is on writing and being writers; she has become a facilitator, an encourager, a guide, and a listener. She feels strongly that it is her job to ensure that meaningful writing is being worked on, that progress is being made, and that a positive writing climate exists.

When working with the students, Jan takes her lead from them. Time was added to the schedule to include more class sharing of written accomplishments. All other assigned writing is completed during project time or other content area time—Jan makes sure that she and the class guard and preserve daily writers' workshop time. She has also become a constant observer. In this way, she learns about and comes to understand each student's writing style, and she can assess how at differing levels and to differing degrees each learner grows in his or her ability to write, to understand the writing process, and to make meaningful written contributions. All of the students demonstrate and articulate their abilities and competencies to be real writers.

It is necessary for Jan as the teacher to guarantee that all the students are supported in their efforts. She has made a commitment to understanding their writing styles and to meeting their writing needs. She knows that both the students and the parent volunteers watch her as she interacts with student writers. Her interactions set a tone, and she wants the message to be clear: writing will be positively supported every day, and this class is an environment that fosters this value.

The freedom to write in writers' workshop has changed the year for everyone—the writers, the parents, and Jan. Writing has become a priority, and the students are proud of their accomplishments and share their stories with constant enthusiasm. They are proud of one another's work, too, and take opportunities to encourage and support one another whenever possible. The climate for writing was not created by Jan; it is a result of giving the students the freedom and room to be engaged in their interests. As writers, they take advantage of the opportunities given them to make daily choices and decisions about their writing; they take their responsibilities seriously and create pieces of a quality that she had never seen when she used an assignment format. Writers' workshop is the combined effort of all of the students as they invest their time and energy in writing, an investment of dedication and caring that makes them true writers.

Students participate as knowledgeable, reflective, creative, and critical members of a variety of literacy communities.

The Last Discussion

The students again sit in a circle on the blue braided rug, involved in a discussion with Jan about writers' workshop. It's near the last day of school, and the children are eager to express their thoughts and ideas about their experiences.

"My favorite part of the whole day was always writers' workshop," LaWanda says.

"I wrote more this year than ever before," Harold chimes in. Other comments abound:

"Writers' workshop was great because I had my own legal pad and folder."

"I liked publishing books and sharing them."

"I really feel like an author because I wrote so much."

"I liked the way my mom would come to help during writers' workshop."

"I was surprised that I could write about what I wanted to write about."

"Being able to work anywhere in the room or in the hall was fun."

"Wait a minute. What about next year?"

And so it goes. These third graders had truly enjoyed the freedom to write. Each of them had become an independent writer capable of communicating in print. Most important, they had learned to *like* writing, and Jan feels that her teaching has meant something—these students will probably use writing throughout their lives, which means their lives will be richer. What more could one ask from education?

What Key Standards Emerge in This Chapter?

Students participate as knowledgeable, reflective, creative, and critical members of a variety of literacy communities.

Jan asks the students to help her think about how to implement writers' workshop in a way that will be effective for everyone in this classroom community. Because the students know that their input is valued and will be listened to seriously, they don't hesitate to share their ideas, and they are invested in their learning. This leads to active engagement on their part. Note how Jan does draw some guidelines for the students so they'll understand the structure in which they'll be participating. She's responsible for providing the framework based on her professional knowledge, and the students then have the room to help fill in specifics in a way they can understand.

Students employ a wide range of strategies as they write and use different writing process elements appropriately to communicate with different audiences for a variety of purposes.

As is evident, Jan and the children are familiar with and discuss different stages of the writing process in their classroom community. Unfortunately, the stages in the writing process are sometimes thought of as steps that have a certain order and build upon one another, which can confine students' writing and thinking unnecessarily. In Jan's classroom, each student has the opportunity to talk about how he or she goes about writing, and that process is valued as an individual one. The stages are more of a way to look at and focus on certain areas of the process, a scaffold to help students be aware in their thinking about writing, rather than a linear confinement. Also, mechanics and grammar are indeed taught and learned—in context, and at the appropriate time. Initially, children are encouraged to get their thoughts and feelings down on paper without worrying about editing, which requires a different type of thinking. As drafts approach the final stage and children know what their piece is about, they are then encouraged to think about making those drafts easier for others to read and to use their editing skills. Editing is not confused with revising, which is a part of the process that requires more global thinking about material. The children and Jan discuss the differences between these stages so that everyone is clear.

Students apply knowledge of language structure, language conventions (e.g., spelling and punctuation), media techniques, figurative language, and genre to create, critique, and discuss print and nonprint texts.

As mentioned above, students do focus on language structure when the time is appropriate to do so. Because they themselves choose to work in different genres such as nonfiction, mysteries, and science fiction, they become familiar with a wide range of possibilities in a way that engages them so they'll retain what they learn. Since parents help with editing in the classroom, students also have a built-in opportunity to share their pieces with different audiences, which helps them look at their work in new ways and want to improve it accordingly.

Students adjust their use of spoken, written, and visual language (e.g., conventions, style, vocabulary) to communicate effectively with a variety of audiences and for different purposes.

Just as the students become familiar with different genres, they become familiar with the purposes of different kinds of writing, which in turn helps them think of audience and the various ways people communicate in general. Publishing their work helps them realize that others consider what they have to say worthwhile, and because of that, they take communication seriously. The students discuss their varying writing styles with one another, and because they share their reactions to others' work, they learn to think about audience more deeply. Sharing their work with one another, with Jan, and with parent volunteers exposes the children to many different kinds of audiences, and the feedback they receive and value helps them to understand the different messages they want and need to get across.

CHAPTER THREE

A TOOLBOX FOR INQUIRY

Earlier we looked into Deb Foertsch's classroom and saw some of the ways she has worked to create an exciting, student-centered environment for reading. We know, however, that in life as well as in most elementary school classrooms, subjects are not so neatly divided. How does the classroom teacher find ways for students to draw connections among the many subjects covered each day, as well as between those subjects and their own lives and interests? And how can we draw on the new technological resources now available to enhance these connections further?

If we had visited Deb's classroom several years ago, we would have seen students in rows reading aloud round-robin style from the text, orally answering text-driven questions Deb asked to check to see if they "got it." Written questions would then be assigned, graded, and returned. A test would be given at the end of each chapter, naturally. And the class would move on. In fact, not only did they go through the school year in this way, but every school day looked similar—moving on schedule from one subject to another (math at 8:30, reading at 10:00, and so on). The plus side of working this way was that students did appear to have equal access to the material they were studying, since, after all, they were reading and discussing it all aloud. Other seeming benefits were that the classroom was quiet and well-organized, and that kids knew what to expect. But just what did they expect? Not a whole lot—just a procession of "subjects" to "get through," a test "to get a good grade on," with a report card received at the end of each quarter in order to show those grades to parents.

It was good to be organized. It was good for kids to have a structure to learn within. It was good for kids to read together. But something didn't feel right to Deb. Was there no time for reflection, for giving real consideration to the important questions which (if encouraged or allowed) might arise from the material the class was sharing? Were there resources beyond the textbook and "old stand-bys" of movies that Deb might be ignoring? Was there a way to move students beyond looking to the teacher not only for all of the answers, but for all of the questions, too? Was there a better way to accommodate the varying abilities, backgrounds, interests, and learning styles of students in the classroom? What are the tools kids need to be successful learners, and how do we help them get these tools?

These were the questions Deb pursued (some of which were there at the beginning, but many of which came as she learned) in order to better her instruction and enhance kids' learning. In order to answer her questions, Deb observed and asked questions of other teachers; attended a multitude of workshops; took university and video courses; read journals, professional magazines, and books; and, more recently, began looking for answers in the great, untamed expanse called cyberspace, using her computer and the Internet. Throughout all of this, Deb jotted down and organized, included and discarded, changed and rearranged, experimented with, practiced, reflected upon, refined, and shared ideas that she'd gathered. Some of what she did she later realized was ludicrous ("Like the time I thought I was teaching a themed, integrated unit on animals because I made sure there was a picture of an animal on every worksheet I assigned," she says). Some of what she learned was right on target ("Like the importance of variety, of choice, of negotiation, of respect, of expecting high standards of performance from kids in their work and in their behaviors, of equal opportunity in learning"). Probably the most important thing Deb learned, however, was to reflect upon *how* she learned and to try to offer kids those same opportunities. Here, then, is a look at where Deb is now in incorporating what she's learned into her classroom.

Developing a Toolbox for Inquiry

The tools for inquiry Deb believes fifth graders need to learn and practice are these:

- identifying interesting and meaningful topics and questions to pursue;
- gathering quality source materials appropriate to their questions, interests, and abilities;
- gleaning information from these sources;
- organizing this information;
- responding to this information;
- sharing what they've learned; and
- pacing themselves for success.

These tools are not taught in isolation, nor are they all to be mastered by the end of the fifth grade. Rather, they are the tools that Deb has found useful to discuss, demonstrate, and integrate into instruction. They are what she focuses on with fifth graders to enable her students to learn how to take responsibility for their own learning.

How can these tools be taught when teachers are also supposed to be teaching everything else under the sun? The best answer Deb has come up with is to use the themed unit. The themed unit is not a new concept, and it certainly doesn't solve all problems. Not everything can be combined into themes. However, themed units do provide students with room for growth and exploration, while encouraging them to look for connections in their learning.

Themed Units: Teaching the Tools and an Attitude for Inquiry

Deb uses a themed unit structure for learning throughout the year. Themed learning facilitates a more connected curriculum; the accommodation of a variety of learning styles, interests, and abilities; the study of ideas from differing viewpoints; the acquisition and practice of literacy strategies; a deeper consideration of important ideas and questions; individual student pursuits and, therefore, responsibility for their own learning; and the building of a community of learners where respect for one another is learned and practiced. Even though the themes are quite varied, the structure of the units remains the same throughout the year, thus providing a flexible framework for learning that becomes familiar and comfortable for students to work within.

When determining which themes to examine with students, Deb considers what topics in the existing curriculum might work well together. (For instance, a hands-on science study of the environment works quite well with a social studies unit on Native American cultures.) Deb also thinks about what is already there in the curriculum that she has to teach that is important, interesting, and able to serve as a springboard to further questioning and study. She then determines the theme and plans the unit components. This plan serves as a beginning for the class's inquiry.

Themed Unit Components

Goals

Important Questions to Begin with and Perspectives to Consider

Available Resources

- school texts (which ones? what page numbers?)
- literature sources (fiction, nonfiction, poetry, etc.)
- media (videos, computer software, movies, music, etc.)
- guest speakers
- field trips
- artifacts

Toolbox Activities

- large-group
- small-group
- individual
- reading
- speaking and listening
- writing

Real Math and Science Connections

- math activities
- science pursuits

Opportunities for Related Learning and Student Choice

Learning Environment

- teacher-created
- student-created

Culminating Celebrations and Product Ideas

Assessment

Some of the ideas Deb first lists under these heads are negotiable with students, while others are not. New component ideas will usually be added by the students. (Examples: "I didn't know that your grandpa participated in the March on Washington! Could he speak to our class about his experience?" or "What a clever idea for a bulletin board! Let's work it up.") Some component ideas Deb will use, and others she won't. All of these components, however, are expanded and blended together to serve as a home base to venture from and return to throughout the class's explorations. Daily lesson plans evolve using this home base list, student responses, student ideas, student needs, and the following structure for unit organization.

Themed Unit Organization: The Structure

The first of these tools for inquiry, identifying interesting and meaningful topics and questions to pursue, is essential. For some kids, this tool comes easily, but for many students it is difficult to learn. Deb believes it is best learned in community. Kids ask questions in class, and these questions serve as a springboard to more questions. Brainstorming and publicly listing questions on a topic, using question writing as homework (with family support), and using idea webs and mind maps are all ways to help students learn to ask questions and identify topics. After lists, webs, and maps have been generated, Deb asks kids to circle the one or two ideas that are "the most important" and then asks them to explain why they chose the topics or questions that they did. These explanations and the discussions that go with them are helpful to students in learning how to pick issues that are important to them.

Gathering Source Materials

Gathering quality source materials appropriate to student questions, interests, and abilities is a tool that is hard for some kids to acquire. We've all had kids who have chosen books on the sole basis of their titles or covers. Then, when it's time to use the books as sources, they're not at all helpful. We've also had kids who accompanied their parents to the library only to return with a source that would be terrific to use in a doctoral dissertation. Deb knows that it's important that kids have practice in finding their own sources (instead of using the book chapter that "Mom photocopied for me at the library"). They also need to be encouraged to feel free *not* to use what doesn't work for them. It's all right to try a source, find it's not working, borrow someone else's to try, and so on. It's also all right to modify a question or topic because a source has helped refocus or redefine ideas.

Deb feels that demonstrating, discussing, and practicing seem to be keys for her students' acquisition of this tool. She and her students talk about what makes a source good: (1) It has to give them information on that question or topic that they didn't know. (2) They have to be able to understand it. (3) It may help them think of something in a new way or

Students conduct research on issues and interests by generating ideas and questions, and by posing problems. They gather, evaluate, and synthesize data from a variety of sources (e.g., print and nonprint texts, artifacts, people) to communicate their discoveries in ways that suit their purpose and audience.

Students participate as knowledgeable, reflective, creative, and critical members of a variety of literacy communities.

Students use a variety of technological and informational resources (e.g., libraries, databases, computer networks, video) to gather and synthesize information and to create and communicate knowledge.

introduce something they hadn't thought of before. When a source doesn't work for one of them, they talk about why it didn't and they try again. They also talk about different kinds of sources—newspapers, computer resources, videos, family members, experts in the field, etc. Many times fifth graders haven't thought about using these as sources. They tend to stick to books and magazines in the beginning. It's also a bit tricky for students to understand how a science experiment, learning simulation, readers theater, or other enjoyable activity can be a good source of information. Once a fellow student ventures out, however, others begin looking beyond print sources. Occasionally Deb has had to put some limitations on these ventures. For example, she had to tell her class that they just didn't have time to "discover" whether Disney's movie *The Little Mermaid* would be a good source for collecting information on squid. But it doesn't matter that she's sometimes had to impose these limits, because they get the point.

Organizing the Information

Deb's class frequently uses graphic organizers to glean information from their sources and to organize this information so that they can work with it. There are many different kinds of graphic organizers to use, so Deb introduces them one at a time throughout the year. She demonstrates the organizer, the class talks about it, kids practice it, and they refer to it again. Kids like some organizers better than others, and they seem to get a better handle on some organizers than on others. However, all the organizers become parts of students' repertoires. Many of these organizers can also double as products to use to share what's been learned. Here are a few of Deb's favorites: description wheel, description chart, outlines, clustering, maps, timelines, compare/contrast chart, Venn diagram, explanation flow-chart, two-column notes, and note-taking on note cards. Kids seem to view these organizers as ways to make the work of handling source information a bit more enjoyable.

Deb doesn't usually simply give students sheets with the organizers on them; instead, students create these for themselves (after Deb or classmates demonstrate them). It seems that drawing the circles, using the rulers for charts, folding the paper, and using grown-up materials like note cards are all very appealing to students.

Responding to the Information

Once the students have gleaned and organized the information, they need to respond to it in some way. This is what makes the learning meaningful for them. It is what they think, feel, believe, understand, or need to understand about the facts that they've organized. Responses can look a number of ways and take a number of forms. Some favorites are responding orally by relating in small groups how this information fits with knowledge, feelings, or experiences students already have; creating a dialogue or writing a letter that discusses the new-found knowledge; listing further questions related to the new learning; commenting on parts of the information that were puzzling or explaining how something was "figured out"; writing opinions expressing different points of view on the information learned; and explaining how what was learned affects the learner's feelings or beliefs. At one workshop Deb attended, the spokesperson, a fellow fifth-grade teacher, spoke about students' writing one-page plays (no narrator allowed; no more than three characters; one page only), and Deb's students have enjoyed using that format for responding. They've also enjoyed writing new words to familiar tunes as a means of response. Of course, many of these response forms can be polished up and used as products, too.

Students apply a wide range of strategies to comprehend, interpret, evaluate, and appreciate texts. They draw on their prior experience, their interactions with other readers and writers, their knowledge of word meaning and other texts, their word identification strategies, and their understanding of textual features (e.g., sound-letter correspondence, sentence structure, context, graphics).

Preparing a Product

When pieces of information have been gleaned, organized, responded to, and joined with other pieces, it's time for students to choose and create products through which to share what they've learned. "To diorama or not to diorama; that is the question!" And how does Deb get students to evaluate their products to make them more effective vehicles for sharing information? She starts out by talking with the class about different products. They talk about what some of the different kinds of products are, and students are asked to choose or create ideas of their own for the products that best showcase their new learning and their talents in presentation. (Thinking about their own talents and timelines is crucial here. If Susie and her partner Lila both hate to draw and letter, a poster would not be a good product choice for them. Perhaps a play would be a better choice. Not that kids shouldn't ever be encouraged to stretch and try new media, but Deb encourages them to use their strengths.) Deb and her students discuss why they chose the products they chose, and then share ideas about how to make the products effective. (Example: Each part of a mobile must be big enough to be readable from a couple of feet away, be two-sided, and be on material that won't curl beyond recognition when it's been hanging around for a day or so. Everyone should be able easily to see that the mobile is a way to share what the student learned and how he or she felt about that learning.) These discussions and demonstrations take quite a bit of time, but the products and sharing that take place are worth it. The class also takes time to applaud, and to evaluate the effectiveness of completed products. This helps learners on their next efforts. Here is a list of products that Deb's class has enjoyed and found worthwhile.

> Students adjust their use of spoken, written, and visual language (e.g., conventions, style, vocabulary) to communicate effectively with a variety of audiences and for different purposes.

diagrams

maps (geographic—real or imaginary)

student-written tests or quizzes

student-created surveys and graphed results

fact files (using note cards)

student-created experiments and lab write-ups

interviews and write-ups

real journals of observations

"pretend" journals of inanimate objects or persons in history

student-created rating scales

tape recordings (audio and video)

learning links—alphabet paper chains on specific topics

fact/opinion note cards (opinion at top and four supporting facts underneath on one side; flip over and do same with opposing viewpoint)

mobiles

data disks

posters (structured!)

folded-paper people biographies

story maps

emotion maps

mind maps

character maps

one-page plays

sketches

lists

annotations

student-created newspapers and magazines

speeches

skits

dialogues

books:

ABC books on different topics

flip-over books

scrapbooks

rubberband books

simple folded-paper books

small one-sheet books

we/me books

photo essays

brown paper bag books (great for collections!)

pop-up books

computer web pages for sharing information with the world

computer spreadsheets and graphs

Pacing the Work

Helping students learn how to pace their work is an important job that needs consistency and patience. Deb's class paces their learning by creating a suggested timeline, as well as assignment notebooks, for completing tasks. Deb also requires regular progress checks on product work, which precludes any "I started over last night so I don't have anything to share today" incidents. Communicating due dates to parents has also proven very useful to students. In fact, communication with parents (in a newsletter, by phone, etc.) is very helpful in supporting students in getting those tools for inquiry. It's important to let parents know how much to help and when not to help and what questions to raise to support kids' learning in and outside of school.

At the beginning of the year, these steps and tools are demonstrated and practiced. As the school year progresses, however, kids become more able to use these tools and this framework for their own pursuits.

The Celebration

This part is always a time for the whole class to reflect upon what they've learned and how they've learned. It's about sharing their learning products. It's about getting the theme's big ideas and posing new questions. It's also about appreciating the efforts that went into their learning and teaching.

Putting It All Together

Toward the beginning of the school year, Deb's class begins a themed unit on "The First Americans." This is a familiar, yet important, theme which lends itself nicely to appreciating different lifestyles and listening to different voices and perspectives. It's a study linking the past with the present in which inter-disciplinary connections can also be made. Archeology and the environment work easily into the study of Native Americans, and there are many activities and sources at many different levels to select and use.

To begin with, Deb "scopes out" the components and jots them onto her sheet. She circles or highlights the "absolutes" on this list. These are her "non-negotiables"—materials and activities she believes are important enough for the whole class to do or learn or take part in. She also leaves blanks, and she writes questions. Then, she places this sheet inside her plan book to use as a guide in daily planning.

Themed Unit Components: "The First Americans"

Goals and General Concepts: environment affecting lifestyles; migration across Bering land bridge; different Native American groups' cultures (compare and contrast); impact of Europeans coming to America; connections to today (portrayals of Native Americans in the media, prejudice, Chief Illini mascot controversy?)

Important Questions to Begin with and Perspectives to Consider: student-generated questions; Native American primary sources and voices

Available Resources:

- school texts (which ones? what page numbers?): history text; supplement: *Adventure Tales of America*
- literature sources (fiction, nonfiction, poetry, etc.): *Sing Down the Moon; Morning Girl; USKids History: Book of the American Indians;* need to find poetry
- media (videos, computer software, movies, music, etc.): Native American Web on Internet; "Five Nations" video segments; check out key-pal possibilities
- guest speakers: check the university
- field trips: local museum program?
- artifacts: co-teacher's fossils; kids' bring-ins

Toolbox Activities

- large-group: chart organizers; asking questions; resource search; product choice
- small-group: partners for product creation and most practice activities
- individual: writing letters as a response; oral tradition response
- reading: whole-group with teacher-selected materials; small-groups/partners with student-selected resources
- speaking and listening: poetry; oral tradition stories
- writing: focus on writing letters

Real Math and Science Connections

- math activities: measuring?
- science pursuits: archeology link; environment study connection

Opportunities for Related Learning and Student Choice: take-home packs on symbolic language and foods; student learning center; minilab on tanning hides; art lessons

Learning Environment
- teacher-created: bulletin board chart to be completed with students
- student-created: art lessons displayed; other ideas?

Culminating Celebrations and Product Ideas: food, music, sharing of products; student ideas?

Assessment: process (observation notes, checklist of toolbox activities); products (oral tradition talks, check of organizers, participation, final product shared)

Introducing the Theme

In introducing the theme of "The First Americans," Deb begins by tossing out the question, "Who were the first Americans?" Everyone knows the answer to this. Discussion continues with Deb's asking questions in response to the students' sharing of what they know about the first Americans. The students know that long ago some Native Americans lived in tepees, hunted buffalo, and wore moccasins. They also seem to understand that there are many Native Americans alive today—that Native American peoples are living now and exist outside of picture and text books. The students say that they think the Native Americans were treated badly by "cowboys" long ago, and they believe that the Native Americans did a better job with respecting the earth than many of us do. Deb asks why they believe this is so, and she listens. Then they shift gears, and Deb asks what they *don't* know about Native Americans. Usually, this is more difficult for fifth graders (believe it or not), so Deb prompts the students and shares some of her own questions when they run a bit dry. Did Native Americans of long ago live in the same general locations and perform about the same everyday activities as their modern descendants? How did they get there to begin with? Is there unfair treatment of Native Americans in society today? Deb asks these questions one at a time and watches the students' puzzlement and interest. Then their own questions and theories come out. Someone believes Native Americans came from South America. Someone else wonders why Europeans and Native Americans didn't "get along." Deb lists these and other questions on the overhead for later use. She closes the introduction by doing a shared reading to provide background information and possibly produce more questions.

Learning Activities: A First-Quarter Sampler on the Theme

The activities described below are representative of different toolbox activities completed early in the school year within Deb's class's study of the First Americans. They are in no particular order and are offered to give a sense of what happens in minilessons and class conversations throughout the unit.

Creation Stories

Gleaning Information: In a whole-class setting, Deb reads one of the creation stories from the *Book of the American Indians*. No one writes, but everyone listens. Deb asks about when this particular story might have been written. All agree that it was probably written long ago. The class then discusses the notion of creation stories, and why they might have been written. The students offer suggestions: maybe for fun (since there were no television programs or movies

Students conduct research on issues and interests by generating ideas and questions, and by posing problems. They gather, evaluate, and synthesize data from a variety of sources (e.g., print and nonprint texts, artifacts, people) to communicate their discoveries in ways that suit their purpose and audience.

Students read a wide range of print and nonprint texts to build an understanding of texts, of themselves, and of the cultures of the United States and the world; to acquire new information; to respond to the needs and demands of society and the workplace; and for personal fulfillment. Among these texts are fiction and nonfiction, classic and contemporary works.

then); maybe to explain how the world came to be (since we "didn't know so much science" then); maybe, some insist, these stories are an explanation of what people believe. Deb then asks them to listen to the same story one more time. "This time it will be different," she tells them. She then retells in her own words the same story that she just read. The kids waste no time in saying that it was the same story except that she only told it this time. Deb asks which version they prefer and gets mixed reviews. Then the class discusses the idea of oral traditions. This is not a totally new idea to the students; they've talked about folk tales in other grades, and how stories change from being handed down by word of mouth.

Response: Deb asks her students whether their own families have oral traditions, stories told again and again. Some hands wave. They want to offer theirs now. Other students say they have none. Deb offers her short version of a story her grandfather used to tell her. This example raises a few more hands. Now it's assignment time, however. Their assignment is to ask at home for one story each that they can share at school as part of their families' oral traditions. The story is to be practiced with the family and with partners in the classroom the next day. All of the stories will be shared in small groups after practice. Sometimes no family tales can be found by a student (some think they have no stories, and some have stories that are just too hard to tell). These hesitant students are then asked if they'd like to retell a story as Deb did in the first lesson. She offers them the book used in that lesson, so that they may read and retell another creation story of their choosing. Of course, they may create their own stories instead.

Informal Sharing and Revisiting: After the stories have been practiced at home, they are shared with class partners. "What makes a story good?" Deb wonders out loud. She jots their ideas on the board—interesting story, vocal expressiveness, eye contact, telling the story in order. These are things to look for. Partners then listen and offer each other "sandwich" critiques—a specific compliment about the partner's rendition, followed by a specific helpful question or suggestion, followed by another specific compliment. "Specific" is the key word here. "Helpful" is another key word. Deb offers good and bad examples of sandwich critiques, and after the students have offered each other their critiques, there's more practice and incorporation of ideas gained from them.

Formal Sharing: This can happen in small or large groups, depending on time available. The students are eager for this, and usually want to share their stories with the whole class because they've worked hard to prepare them. Sometimes, if not too much class time has been used for practicing and critiquing, they share the stories in small groups instead. The students all enjoy this and learn a lot about one another.

Sing Down the Moon: An Ongoing Activity

The book *Sing Down the Moon*, by Scott O'Dell, is shared by the whole class because it's a book Deb wants all of her fifth-grade students to experience and have in common. They read and discuss the book aloud in large group, small groups, and with partners; they read it quietly on their own in school and at home. (Variety is the spice of a fifth grader's life—and this allows for modeling and multiple opportunities to support struggling readers.)

Gathering and Organizing Information: As the members of the class read this rich and descriptive book, they keep two charts. One chart is kept for and by the whole class, and a different kind of chart is kept by each individual student. At

Students adjust their use of spoken, written, and visual language (e.g., conventions, style, vocabulary) to communicate effectively with a variety of audiences and for different purposes.

Students read a wide range of literature from many periods in many genres to build an understanding of the many dimensions (e.g., philosophical, ethical, aesthetic) of human experience.

the end of each episode, the class illustrates it, summarizes it in a few sentences, and records it on the class chart. They do this as a class because it is early in the school year, and Deb wants this summarizing and organizing demonstrated for everyone. Usually, they talk about what's to be recorded, and then Deb has volunteers do the writing and illustrating some time during the day. Before beginning a new section of text, the class uses the chart as a recap of where they've been in the book and as a springboard to where they're going.

Response: The charts kept by individual students look like the whole-class chart, but are not used the same way. The students' own charts are a type of "empathy" chart, which the class calls "heart charts." For each episode charted by the whole class, students are to choose one character and write and illustrate how they believe that character felt during that episode and why they believe the character felt that way. This helps students to try to identify with the different characters, to get into their hearts and look at what makes them "real." It also provides perspective on several devastating events in Native Americans' history, in our country's history.

Sharing: The class shares and uses the class chart as they go, and they marvel at their work and at the book upon the chart's completion. However, heart charts are not usually shared, except at the student's discretion. Lots of kids like to share these. Others don't. Deb doesn't do a sharing event for this, other than class conversation.

The Facts of the Matter: Using the Gathered Materials

Usually students are quick to bring in materials from home and elsewhere that they have determined to be on the theme or potentially helpful in addressing their general topic of interest. But what can be done with all of the materials they bring? How can the search be made worthwhile?

Sharing Resources: As materials are being gathered, kids are eager to share the resources they've found. They do this at first informally with their small groups, with other classmates, and with Deb. Deb doesn't organize this sharing. It just seems to happen. It's always surprising how many kids know what one another's materials are before they formally share that information. It is important that each child in the class bring in a source to use. All need to feel a responsibility for gathering the materials, and Deb quietly makes sure every student has something there. Once everyone has brought in a resource (and Deb will give a deadline for this, if need be) the first thing they do as a class is a formal, organized sharing about what materials are in the room, as each student *briefly* shows the source materials he or she has brought.

In the case of the "First Americans" theme, there's usually quite a variety. Besides many books at varying levels of readability and interest from the library, there are vacation pictures, jewelry, a special blanket sent by a mother's pen pal, and souvenir booklets. The class shares what's in the room so that each student knows what resources are available besides his or her own. Books become "Sue's book with the Kachina doll information" or "Bryan's book about the Trail of Tears," which personalizes the exchange of information and makes just the having of the resource materials important. Artifacts, once shared, become

Students use a variety of technological and informational resources (e.g., libraries, databases, computer networks, video) to gather and synthesize information and to create and communicate knowledge.

Students participate as knowledgeable, reflective, creative, and critical members of a variety of literacy communities.

sources for topics. Deb wondered aloud, for example, about the pen pal relationship and what made the blanket so special, and was told that it was "handmade by my mom's pen pal's friend." How was such a beautiful blanket made? A topic takes shape not just for Lisa, who brought in the artifact, but also for her friend Tyonna. The class also now knows who can help them out on a selected topic if their own materials end up not being as helpful as they had expected. Even though Tim hasn't been especially good friends with Jason, he's eager to borrow or share Jason's book on Cochise. Sharing of resources is a powerful way to bring kids together who might or might not have chosen each other's company at first. Using the resources, original questions, and interests, the students narrow and define more closely those beginning individual topics and questions, with Deb's guidance.

Gathering Information: Once topics or questions have been defined, the difficult process of getting information from the various print sources begins. Deb first uses one of the student's sources to illustrate the problems they face. She shows what it looks like to copy straight from the book, and when she asks what problem she's showing, the kids all know that she's copying. Then Deb shows what writing too much information looks like, then too little, then the right amount but not on the selected topic. The kids love these "bad examples," and they learn as much from them as when Deb next demonstrates a "good example." She tells them there are many different ways to get information from print, and that the way she's showing them at that point is just one of those.

Then Deb demonstrates choosing a part of the book that might be helpful to her (using the table of contents and index); reading that section of the book one "chunk" at a time; and closing the book and writing down important information or big ideas that she remembers (and no, it's not cheating to look back for spellings or more ideas). Deb jots her information onto the overhead, along with the title, page number(s), and author of the book she is using. Since this is a big lesson with a lot to remember, Deb will demonstrate each step again, and this time stop after each part to let students try each step with the books they brought. She has them do this practicing in partners, which really seems to help. She also limits the number of facts the students are to write ("no more than six ideas"). Sticking to the topic or question is tough for fifth graders, especially if the book they're using is full of interesting information. Because their attention is easily diverted from their original pursuit, having narrowly defined questions to answer or a topic to address, and a limit on the number of ideas they can record, seems to help resolve this dilemma.

Though they will do two-column notes or writing on note cards later in the year, for now Deb has the students write on notebook paper. The next lesson will be a quick review of this one, with plenty of time allowed for partners to write information and for Deb to move around the room and support those kids needing help.

Organizing the Information: Since this is a difficult skill, especially at the beginning of fifth grade, Deb has the students circle their three most interesting pieces of information and write them in complete sentences onto a sheet she provides. Each piece of information is illustrated, and placed with other classmates' sheets into a class book. This fulfills the need for some instant feedback and provides a way to look at all that has been learned and accomplished already.

Revisiting and Reorganizing: For this early theme, the product is the information organizer. Since the class book has been created as a model, students

— Students apply a wide range of strategies to comprehend, interpret, evaluate, and appreciate texts. They draw on their prior experience, their interactions with other readers and writers, their knowledge of word meaning and other texts, their word identification strategies, and their understanding of textual features (e.g., sound-letter correspondence, sentence structure, context, graphics).

use their own notes to organize and create individual student books. The topic or question each of them has chosen to address becomes the title of the book.

It is at this point that many students go back into their notes and resource materials in order to make sure they have good information to share with others and to make sure that they've stayed on the topic. It is also at this point that some students will get "stuck." They can't find the answer to their particular question or they took more notes than needed on a topic and are confused. This is the time for Deb's input—helping students get "unstuck" by, for example, allowing them to change topics, guiding them to other resources, or helping them to define what in a source is important to them and their topic.

Once students write the facts from their notes in complete sentences onto construction paper pages, they illustrate the pages, place them in a logical order, and create a cover page. Deb then makes them into individual spiral-bound books for sharing.

The Celebration and Reflection

Individual books are shared with the class, one at a time. All efforts are applauded, and students comment on what made their fellow classmates' books effective. As the books are being shared, students listen carefully. In addition to enjoying one another's work, students also have on their desks in front of them individual copies of the class questions generated at the beginning of the unit. This revisiting of their old questions reinforces the important practice of listening to one another for new understandings.

After all have shared their individual products and all have been applauded and celebrated, they take a hard look at their learning in a class discussion. Can they now answer all of the questions they had at the beginning of their unit? Which questions could be explored further? How do they know their answers are correct? Did they gain new perspectives? Did they hear all voices? Were they fair in their answers? How do their new understandings make a difference in their own lives? Are there other pursuits that they might want to learn about on their own? Where else can their new learning take us?

Many times the end-of-unit celebrations in Deb's class include food, music, and entertainment in the form of sharing student products. However, a very important part of these celebrations is the reflection. It's imperative that students know that even though a unit has ended, their learning has not.

Putting the "Logical" into "Technological"

Last spring, Deb's school district offered teachers an opportunity to write a grant in order to obtain computer equipment for their classrooms. Fortunately, hers was one of the grants funded. The requests were not to exceed a certain dollar amount, so Deb had asked for one computer with display equipment. (That way, she could show the computer's wonders and give computer instruction to her whole class at one time, without having to arrange for or give individualized instruction each time a different student was to use the computer for a new task.) In December, Deb came across a boxed computer in the hallway with her name on it. After checking to make sure it was indeed hers, Deb shoved the box down the hall to rest in her classroom until it could be set up and installed with software.

Students participate as knowledgeable, reflective, creative, and critical members of a variety of literacy communities.

Already, Deb's "wheels were spinning" with the teaching possibilities of this magic-machine-in-a-box. Deb had taken several computer courses through the University of Illinois's National Center for Supercomputing Applications, and so she was familiar with e-mail, word processing, and the Internet's World Wide Web. As she was daydreaming about the new computer, her students were filing into the classroom from lunch. It didn't take long before they, too, were reeling with the possibilities of a computer in the classroom. While she had been visualizing her classroom being connected to "the outside world," pondering and exploring great ideas over the Internet (much like those commercials one sees on television), her students had been visualizing quite another scene.

"Mrs. Foertsch, can I bring in my Myst game? It could be really educational for everyone. After all, you have to read and really think in order to win."

"Does this mean we can play Oregon Trail? I played that game at my cousin's, and we shot six buffalo before we died. And it ties in with learning history, too."

It was clear to Deb that she would have to do some further heavy-duty thinking and planning in order to incorporate the computer into her classroom effectively.

The Computer in the Classroom: What It Won't Be

After that initial, clumsy introduction, Deb proceeded to define for herself what part the new computer would play and, just as important, wouldn't play in her classroom. It was easier for her to define what she didn't want it to be.

The computer in the classroom should not be a time waster. Deb was not going to put students on the computer to play games more reinforcing of "hand-eye coordination" than of learning. She was also not going to use the computer to have students drill isolated skills. After all, she tried to make her teaching connected, and she wasn't going to let a computer (and the myriad skill-and-drill software programs available) sway her convictions about how kids learn best. She also wasn't going to allow students to play their way through what could be potentially powerful learning simulations, like Oregon Trail. Such a program is an example of software from which kids could learn a lot, with guidance. Without guidance, it could be a time waster—a game for them to see how many buffalo they could "shoot."

The computer in the classroom should not be a replacement. It should not be a replacement for books. (Deb loves the sound of kids turning pages during silent reading, and to her there's just something about the feel of a good book.) Nor should the computer and its capabilities replace paper and pencil in the classroom. E-mail and word processing could never take the place of that hand-written letter or thoughtfully written note. Finally, the computer in the classroom should not replace the teacher, although at times Deb admits that "virtual" teaching would be nice. Ah! To "teach" over the computer while at home with a fireplace and a cup of coffee close at hand! As tempting as that may seem, Deb doesn't see it being effective in reality.

The Computer in the Classroom: What It Will Be

Knowing what the computer would not be in Deb's classroom was a help to defining what it could be. The only limitations here are imposed by lack of money, lack of knowledge about current technological capabilities, and lack of time to take part in computer projects, programs, or research that could lead to bigger and better uses for computers in the classroom.

Computers in Deb's classroom will be used for communication. The class will use e-mail for asking experts questions, sharing ideas, and participating in projects with other classes around the globe. They'll take "virtual field trips" on the World Wide Web to museums and other web sites that connect to their units of study and inquiry, and they'll communicate with other schools using the computer and video link-ups. They'll create their own World Wide Web homepage to share their learning with others. Cyberspace is full of possibilities for learning!

Computers in Deb's classroom will also be used for production. Kids will create multimedia products to share what they've learned. Desktop publishing software gives students the opportunity to make polished newsletters, and word-processing programs facilitate the writing process for fifth graders who dislike revising and editing. Spreadsheets can be completed by students to organize and manipulate data and information. Timelines can be created to tie in with their study of U.S. history.

Computers in the classroom will also be used for meaningful simulations. In addition to "Oregon Trail," there are a number of other software programs that can facilitate kids' learning through "experiencing what it's like." For these simulations to be truly meaningful, direction and guidance are needed, but simulations offer many possibilities for broadening students' understanding.

Finally, computers in the classroom will be used as a teacher's tool. Imagine teaching about revising writing by using a word-processing program with the class. Instead of laboriously writing class stories on the overhead, Deb can easily type the story as students dictate it, and then reword and even move entire paragraphs to demonstrate revising. Instead of just talking about Japan in an author study of Yoshiko Uchida, Deb can "take the class" to a web site to check out a Japanese school's schedule of events. The class can go back in time to visit some primary sources that have been placed online and that can enhance their study of the American Revolution. Also, Deb can use the computer as a record-keeping tool, keeping anecdotal records and grades online. The computer also provides ample opportunity for the creation of teacher-made, professional-looking exams, graphic organizers, study sheets, etc.

Now What?

Once Deb had defined what the computer would not and would be used for in her classroom, what did she do? First, she's learned to have patience. It takes time to learn about different pieces of software, and it takes even more time to prepare multimedia lessons or to locate worthwhile web sites that facilitate instruction. (It's worth the time it takes, but lots of time and effort can be spent in the searching.) One also has to be patient when it comes to the money part. Technological tools—both hardware and software—are a major expense. One always has to make the best use of what one has. But isn't that the way it's always been in teaching?

Students use a variety of technological and informational resources (e.g., libraries, databases, computer networks, video) to gather and synthesize information and to create and communicate knowledge.

Students employ a wide range of strategies as they write and use different writing process elements appropriately to communicate with different audiences for a variety of purposes.

Although patience is important, Deb has learned that it's just as important to "dive in" to using the technology she does have. Learning how to use the computer can be very intimidating and, at times, frustrating. However, it's important that teachers use all of the teaching tools they have. It's also important that inservice education be offered to support teachers' use of technology in the classroom.

In Deb's classroom, what she's done is this:

1. Deb incorporates the computer into at least one lesson per day. When she uses the computer as a teaching tool, she reviews, in the context of a lesson, the computer skills students need in order to use the computer effectively on their own. For example, she demonstrated using the spelling checker in a review of a piece the class had written together a day earlier. Then, she expects students to use the skills she has demonstrated in their individual time on the computer. In this case, students were to run the spelling checker during their editing of "special person" essays they'd written on the computer a week earlier.

2. Deb keeps the computer busy with students using it at almost all times during the school day. Students are assigned what to do on the computer, and a class list is kept nearby for record keeping. When a student has completed the computer assignment, he or she checks off and dates the box near his or her name. Then it's that student's job to notify the next person on the list. This has proven to be a pretty efficient system for Deb's one-computer classroom. No student may spend over half an hour at a time on the computer assignment. On cold days, during inside recess, two students are allowed to use the "paint" or "draw" programs for fun. Right now, Deb's students are working on a fifth-grade logo to be used in the creation of their homepage on the World Wide Web.

3. Deb's class and their parents have been made aware of their district's user policies. Internet permission slips have been signed by the students' parents, and instruction on the Internet has been integrated into Deb's lessons in order to prepare students to pass a test on the Internet and gain their "Internet driver's licenses." The class took the test just a few weeks after the arrival of the computer, and most of them passed this district exam on the first try.

Technology opens up a realm of possibilities for both teachers and students. Of course, these possibilities are accompanied by a number of questions to be explored. How to assure equal access to the new technology? How to keep up with the rapidly changing world of technology? How (and when during an already-packed day) to give students the tools they need to use the new technology properly and wisely (everything from keyboarding skills to word-processing know-how to accessing the Internet)? How and when do teachers learn to use the new technologies themselves, as educators? Who will maintain the equipment, and how? How will this all be afforded?

Stepping Back, Looking In

Deb's goal is for kids to have gained several things (not necessarily in any order) upon completing a unit of study: (1) Knowledge: Did they learn information or facts from the unit that they can use and build on in future studies or apply to their own lives? (2) Process: Did they learn a process (how to obtain that information or organize that information) that they can use in the future? (3) Attitude: Did they care about what they learned? Did they think about a new perspective or have their beliefs about the world confirmed or changed in any way? Will this make a difference in their lives today or in the future?

Ideally, all the students have gained some new information, a new way to think about and organize that information, and some new insight. Personal learning has occurred for kids when they use the strategy again and when they show they care on the playground or at home about what they discussed in class.

Personal learning and inquiry are encouraged when students are as active as possible in determining what happens. Even if students have no say-so about the "official" lesson, Deb sees it as her job to reach them in her teaching. That means she thinks about their energy levels, their readiness to engage in the prepared activity, and ways to relate it to the needs and interests they bring into the classroom with them. Deb also tries hard to involve kids in choosing materials, projects, and topics, to incorporate their interests, and to be flexible. Giving students opportunities for learning and exploring on their own and in groups is very important, and student choice is a powerful way to teach. All students deserve an equal opportunity to explore questions, share ideas, and make their voices heard.

What Key Standards Emerge in This Chapter?

Students read a wide range of print and nonprint texts to build an understanding of texts, of themselves, and of the cultures of the United States and the world; to acquire new information; to respond to the needs and demands of society and the workplace; and for personal fulfillment. Among these texts are fiction and nonfiction, classic and contemporary works.

The beauty of Deb's students' engagement with inquiry is that it draws on, and highlights connections among, informational texts and imaginative texts in many different media and from many different eras. Through seeking out, choosing, reading, and sharing these texts Deb's students learn a great deal about our country's history, current issues, and their own values and ideas.

Students conduct research on issues and interests by generating ideas and questions, and by posing problems. They gather, evaluate, and synthesize data from a variety of sources (e.g., print and nonprint texts, artifacts, people) to communicate their discoveries in ways that suit their purpose and audience.

As Deb recognized early in her teaching career, learning only becomes meaningful for students, in fact may only really be learning at all, when it responds to their own questions, needs, and interests. While Deb, like all of us, begins with certain essential material to be covered, she creates an environment in which students take ownership of that material, building on what they already know and believe about it to explore what they need or want to learn. The genuine inquiry that develops then naturally encompasses sources both within and outside of the classroom as learners seek out a wide variety of sources for information and insights.

Students use a variety of technological and informational resources (e.g. libraries, databases, computer networks, video) to gather and synthesize information and to create and communicate knowledge.

Deb realizes that the burgeoning of new sources of information, many of which require increasing sophistication to find and evaluate, presents one of the greatest challenges to educators aiming to foster full literacy in their students. Deb's class is lucky in having a computer with online access, which Deb is striving to incorporate as fully as possible into her students' learning. Deb also realizes that the best way to introduce students to a wide range of informational resources is to encourage and focus their natural curiosity (turning "Oregon Trail" from a game into a tool for genuine learning, for instance), while helping them to develop clear strategies for seeking out and critically evaluating such resources.

Students participate as knowledgeable, reflective, creative, and critical members of a variety of literacy communities.

Deb's whole plan for her class is built on students' drawing on one another, and not just on her, for ideas, criticism, and encouragement at every stage. Students appreciate and evaluate one another's resources, critique and enjoy one another's stories, and spark one another's questions and excitement about learning through whole-class discussions, small-group work, joint work on products, and involvement with literacy communities at school, at home, in their neighborhoods, towns, and cities, and online. Throughout the year students are learning to speak to, and equally important listen to, a variety of perspectives and voices both inside and outside of the classroom.

Students use spoken, written, and visual language to accomplish their own purposes (e.g., for learning, enjoyment, persuasion, and the exchange of information).

Once Deb's students become fully engaged in posing and pursuing their own questions, and in seeking out their own sources of information, their learning has become truly their own and has expanded beyond the classroom and beyond this particular "unit" with its final grade. Deb's students now connect what they are learning in school with their own interests, needs, and values, and have gained the confidence and the skills for lifelong growth in literacy.

References

Potts, Jody. (1993). *Adventure tales of America: An illustrated history of the United States 1492–1877.* Illus. F. Lisenby and J. D. Poole. Dallas: Signal Media.

Bovert, H. E., and Baranzini, M. S. (1994). *USKids history: Book of the American Indians.* Illus. T. T. Bruce. New York: Little, Brown.

Dorris, M. (1992). *Morning girl.* New York: Hyperion Books for Children.

O'Dell, S. (1970). *Sing down the moon.* Boston: Houghton Mifflin.

CHAPTER FOUR

WANTING TO KNOW THE WAYS INTO MULTIAGE

This is how it begins. Imagine that you have been a teacher for twenty-one years, and that you're quite comfortable teaching fourth grade, which you've done for some time now (if you are being described here and don't even have to imagine, all the better). It's the end of the school year, and, just as you're planning what to do with the summer, you're told that because enrollment in the district has decreased dramatically you and two of your colleagues will be expected to teach a multiage grouping of eight-, nine-, and ten-year-olds the following academic year.

You have a choice. You could panic, then become angry, and say, "That's it. I've had enough," and find a job in another district or leave the profession altogether. Or, after the initial shock wears off, you could look at the situation as an opportunity to think in new ways about learning, take a deep breath, plunge in, trust your instincts, and stretch yourself professionally in ways you never imagined possible. After all, you're a teacher, a good one, one who believes that his or her most important responsibility is to the children. This happened to Stephanie Sierra, but her story and the story of the students in her multiage classroom at Oakwood Elementary School in Elyria, Ohio, could just as easily be any teacher's, and we can learn from it.

Professional Knowledge, Community, and Culture

A journey into broader and deeper knowledge often begins in the way Stephanie's did. We are given a challenge, and in order to meet it, we use our imaginations to open up our thinking and stretch our vision. Even though sometimes we're not aware that we're doing so, we assess what we know and believe, and compare that to what we need to learn. Because it's important to know our strengths and to become aware of our teaching philosophies, the following exercise is one worth experimenting with.

Stephanie takes time to reflect on what she is learning and on her teaching philosophy regularly. In her journal, she writes, "I am a good teacher. What makes me one?" She lists all those qualities that are important to her: listening; caring about making children's lives better; her own life story, which has helped her be more sensitive to those children who might otherwise be lost; her intelligence and curiosity; her ability to learn from the children; her love of reading and writing; her conviction that children learn more when they can apply their knowledge concretely to their lives and when the learning experience is enjoyable. She then writes, "I don't yet have the questions to guide me in this unknown territory of multiage education. Who or what can I look to?"

She talks first with her colleagues—since they're all dealing with similar fears, concerns, and, yes, a little excitement, it's important that they discuss their thoughts with one another and help one another come up with creative solutions that will work for them in their own ways. Too often teachers work in isolation, which does both them and their students a disservice. How much richer our learning experience is when we have the opportunity to talk with others about it! And how powerful—there's nothing like finally being able to discuss a fear or insecurity we think no one else struggles with, only to find that others struggle with it as well; we're able then to build our confidence, overcome that insecurity, and appreciate our strengths. But when we work in isolation, all too often our fears build up, we become defensive, we risk burnout, and we miss out on very important opportunities to grow and enrich our professional lives.

The NCTE/IRA *Standards for the English Language Arts* are meant to provide us with guiding principles about good, solid education, and are another way for Stephanie and her colleagues to make sense out of the new world they'll be encountering. This chapter talks about how Stephanie used her professional instincts and then gained broader and deeper insight by relying on her colleagues, the standards, and the wealth of professional literature available.

This is often the reality of how we begin to grow. We're faced with a situation that we must resolve for ourselves in one way or another. We have a hunch about what might work, and so we think about how to implement our ideas. We give ourselves permission to stumble, to get up, and to try again, and, most important, we listen to and watch children closely in order to understand what it is they're trying to tell us.

Stephanie knew she would have to rethink many of her assumptions about the classroom. To get a sense of the way students interact in school areas outside the classroom, she looked to the playground, knowing she could find a wealth of information there if she was open to it. She watched how children of different ages played together, which made her wonder why classrooms were divided into same-age groups in the first place. In turning to professional literature written by other educators, she discovered that on their own children tend to gather in groups of different ages 55 percent of the time, and in same-age groups only 6 percent of the time (Ellis, Rogoff, and Cromer 1981, qtd. in McClellan 1994, 147). Stephanie breathed a sigh of relief and actually got excited. Awaiting her and her future students was an environment as

naturally conducive to learning as possible, and it would be up to her to use her expertise to help create a rich world for her students that they would take with them.

Stephanie's newly gained knowledge about age grouping, combined with what she knew about the way the human mind develops and how important a sense of community is to children, enabled her to envision how her classroom might work. Once the sense of community was established, she knew she'd need to reflect its importance in the way children learned; everyone must be able to contribute to the class in his or her own way. Therefore, small-group work would be important, as would students' having the freedom to choose projects and share their accomplishments. Children of varying abilities and ages needed to be near one another and work together so that all members of the class could learn and feel valued and respected. Students would share in literary discussions, and there would be plenty of group projects that would enable students to participate confidently. Stephanie wanted democracy in her classroom; she wanted her students to thrive. She came across a sentence that struck a chord with her: "As teachers often have noted, in the process of teaching one also consolidates and deepens one's own understanding. Likewise, children who tutor another child have been found to increase the depth and organization of their own knowledge" (Bargh and Shul 1980, qtd. in McClellan 1994, 159). Here was her key. The students would have the opportunity to teach one another, older and younger, just as she would learn from them and they from her. Therefore, it was important that she have a classroom not only of different ages, but of different abilities, with as equal a distribution as possible of boys and girls. She got on the phone and got to work. Her summer began.

In the fall, Stephanie hoped she was ready—she was certainly more excited and nervous than she'd been in a long time. Even though the students would guide her and help one another, the reality was also that she carried a big responsibility. According to Diane E. McClellan, "It is important to be clear that in a multiage classroom, as in any classroom, the role of the teacher is very important. . . . The teacher must know how to help . . . children examine and test out their ideas. . . . In particular, the teacher needs to model a stance of respect so the younger or less experienced child has the confidence to fully articulate his or her own ideas" (1994, 158). Further, her classroom needed to have a very clear sense of an underlying structure if her students were to feel free to explore and take risks, and they all needed to negotiate what that structure would be. (See the class's schedule on page 58.) In short, she needed to know not only what she was doing but why she was doing it.

Once Stephanie understood the social foundations important to learning, she was ready to think about how content could best be taught, to think about the broad framework of her and her students' curriculum. Since writing and reading are at the heart of knowing and learning, she chose to focus on these areas first.

Writing

One of Stephanie's most important questions for herself, as it is for all of us, was "How can I help students achieve their writing potential?" In a rapidly changing world where literacy is becoming more and more important in order for citizens to function successfully, this question is one that must be asked, and one that merits a great deal of thought on the teacher's part. The writing environment must of course be safe—students need to feel free to experiment with their writing and be encouraged to take risks, and they need the time to explore and communicate what is important to them. Donald Graves, in his most recent book, *A Fresh Look at Writing* (1994), argues that essential conditions for effective writing to take place in the classroom are: time, choice, response, demonstration, expectation, room structure, and evaluation. Another condition—trust—would be essential in Stephanie's classroom; without trust, students would not feel free to experiment and become better writers.

Stephanie's school is Target-Assisted, which means that the students traditionally have not done well, and that the population is diverse, generally from families who do not have some of the advantages of those who might be middle- or upper-class. Therefore, trust is of the essence—if students are to understand and support one another's differences, if they're to feel they can learn and do their best, everyone in the community needs to feel safe to do so. Too often, these are the children who receive the message that they will always be the ones left behind. Stephanie knew that if she focused immediately and solely on pointing out errors in spelling, punctuation, capitalization, and the like, the children would be silenced and learn to avoid writing, which would mean they would also learn that it would be safer not to think on their own. This is not the legacy she wanted for them. So she thought long and hard about the conditions in her school and outside, about her own teaching style, and about the expectations of her students, her students' parents, her principal, and the community at large. What would work best for her classroom? The students, of course, would help determine that, but nonetheless she needed to come up with some ideas to start with.

Time

From 9:30 to 10:30 every morning, Stephanie and her students write their own stories, research projects, have minilessons on the writing process and mechanics, confer with one another, and edit their work. Because time is made for writing every day in the schedule, the message to the students is that writing is important.

Choice

The students are free to write whatever is of interest to them, and they're very often inspired by what they see their peers doing. If they become "stuck," Stephanie helps by asking questions such as, "What happened yesterday that you're still thinking about?" or, "Tell me what you feel good about, what you really like to do." If the answer is, as it can be, "Nothing," Stephanie persists. She knows the children in her classroom, so she can help guide them in knowing their strengths. Whether they can hit home runs or take good care of pets or teach younger siblings or draw or find their way around the city, Stephanie is quick to point out what every individual has to offer. It helps the children become excited both about their writing and about their own sense of self.

Students use spoken, written, and visual language to accomplish their own purposes (e.g., for learning, enjoyment, persuasion, and the exchange of information).

Response

Sometimes, especially during the initial drafts of a piece, students need to hear simply that they're doing well and that they just need to keep going without Stephanie getting in the way. At other times, they need specific strategies and

8:20–8:35 Bell rings. Students enter classroom, sharpen pencils, and arrange their desks. Attendance, Pledge, Song, Calendar

8:35–9:05 *Drop Everything and Read (DEAR)*
Stephanie keeps a record of books students read. If students are not yet ready to choose their own books, she chooses for them. During this time, students may read out loud to Stephanie, a Title I teacher, a teacher's aide, a community volunteer, a tape recorder, or one another.

9:05–9:30 *Responding to Literature*
At least three times a week, (two times a week during the second semester), students respond to the books being read, writing in spiral-bound notebooks called "daybooks." If they need more time to read with Stephanie or an aide, time is allotted to support them. If students have already responded, they may use this time to write to pen pals or to write a story or poem.

9:30–10:00 *Writing*
Students write every day, and about three times a week an editing lesson is given to teach writing mechanics. This is of course taught in context, according to the needs Stephanie observes in her students' writing processes.

10:00–10:30 *Literary/Literacy Focus*
Students are encouraged to write their own stories, research projects, or engage in any other literary/literacy activity the class needs to focus on. Often, literary circles, book sharing, writing conferences, and the like are taking place during this time.

10:30–11:20 *Math*
Students use math journals to log problems, problem-solving strategies, or any other math activities pertinent to them.

11:20–11:35 *Recess*
11:35–11:45 *Retelling of Read-Aloud Book*
11:45–12:15 *Lunch*

12:15–12:45 *Read Aloud*
Stephanie reads a book to the students, demonstrating reading expression, literary sharing, and ways to respond to literature. This process reinforces ways students can respond to literature in their daybooks. Stephanie shows them how to respond via a letter, a character web, a picture, a caption, and any other ways that might reach particular students. Later on, Stephanie and the students develop a Reading Response Guide, which helps everyone think more clearly and critically in responses.

12:45–1:30 *Social Studies/Science/Health*
Students research their chosen topics, which may be about famous Americans, holidays around the world, the United States, Ohio history, planets, magnets, electricity, oceans, plants, animals, the human body, diseases, drugs, and friendships, to name just a few! They use a variety of materials to gather information; for example, they write letters to physicians and meteorologists, bring in newspapers, and read magazines and books.

1:30–2:00 *Flexible Time*
Students either continue to work on their research, or they may choose to meet with their Kindergarten Reading Buddies or work on the class newspaper. Guest speakers come in to talk about local government—whether it be the mayor, the state representative, or a parent who may be a city council member. Other community members speak to the class about the importance of reading and writing, and how they use those skills in their jobs. A guest speaker is usually invited two or three times per month.

2:00–2:15 *Home-School Journal*
An important home-school connection, the journal is intended to give students an opportunity to write about important school events during the day. Usually, the entry consists of a page written about a school activity that means something to the student. On Thursdays, the children write two questions relating to an event that occurred; these questions are open-ended and are intended to involve parents or caretakers in the child's school life. Adults read the events described for the week and respond to the questions. On Mondays, students bring their home-school journals to the classroom and begin the process again.

Students employ a wide range of strategies as they write and use different writing process elements appropriately to communicate with different audiences for a variety of purposes.

suggestions, which Stephanie will help them figure out. She feels it's important for the children to develop a language that makes sense to them in thinking about writing; that way, they learn to develop more sophisticated questions to ask themselves and one another during their writing processes. Often, Stephanie will name what she sees a student doing well ("You chose strong words here to describe your cat, Anthea; instead of saying 'Marvin is cute and funny,' you said, 'Marvin has two big black spots around his eyes and he jumps in the air for no reason'") and then she'll ask what the student wants to do to become an even better writer. If the student can't answer, Stephanie will provide some suggestions, but it's important that the student have the chance to think things through first. Sometimes she'll ask students to read their pieces out loud to her, because it often helps them hear what they might miss reading by sight alone. Whatever the strategy, it's important that Stephanie's suggestions aren't rote. The students need to know that she is invested in what they're trying to accomplish at a particular time, and it's only that way that Stephanie can be connected to what a particular student may need.

Demonstration

Children watch adults, and they watch them closely. Stephanie realized the importance of writing in front of her students and along with them in their learning environment. She knew that if she wanted to challenge them to think about the true purpose of writing—to communicate what the writer is interested in—so that they and their readers would be engaged and feel they had something of value to say, she needed to demonstrate what writers do and how they think. In other words, she needed to be a writer, too, which scared her. But what kind of teacher would she be if she didn't take a risk along with her students? How could she help students overcome their fears of writing if she couldn't overcome her own? By experiencing what they experienced, she would gain insight that she could gain no other way.

Expectation

Stephanie was not willing to settle for second best when it came to her kids. From experience, she knew what both low and high expectations from an adult can do to or for a child. When she was in first grade, she took out her first library book, and she was in awe of the process. Her mother and father valued reading, and she'd grown up hearing the folktales and stories of her grandmother and aunts, spoken in the magical rhythm of Spanish. Now she had a book to read, all her own, signed out to her. It was an awesome responsibility, to take care of this book. Unfortunately, one of her many cousins (Stephanie's family is very close), took a crayon and defaced the book, not understanding the implications of what he'd done. When Stephanie discovered what had happened, she was afraid to tell her parents—not only because she knew how upset they'd be that the book had been ruined, but more because she didn't want to get her little cousin into trouble. So she lied. She said that she'd lost the book, and took not living up to her responsibility in caring for it very hard.

Sound like a little thing? Because of that one incident, Stephanie associated books with feeling bad. Because of that one incident, Stephanie did not become an enthusiastic reader until she was in high school.

But in high school, she had teachers who were able to coax her out of her protective shell, teachers who introduced her to the world of story again. Because of her teachers' love for good books and their understanding of how Stephanie had felt for years, and their knowledge of how to reach her, Stephanie learned—in the true sense of the word—how to read. And to think. And to expand her horizons. And to articulate her values. She saw the power of good teaching and how it lasts for a student's lifetime, and that's the kind of impact she wanted to make.

Therefore, she would make it clear to her own students that she believed they could make great strides with their writing. Paying attention to her own story helped her gain more insight into how to be a better teacher.

Room Structure

Books, good books, needed to be everywhere. We cannot write well without reading good writing, and so Stephanie makes sure she has an ample supply of fiction, nonfiction, poetry, picture books, and chapter books, on shelves and in milkcrates throughout the room. When children are surrounded by books, they learn the value and pleasure in reading, which connects to the value and pleasure in writing. In one corner is a comfortable space where students gather to talk about their writing—what worked, what didn't, what's learned—and some of what is discussed is written down and put on a bulletin board to share with other students should they come across a similar experience. Another bulletin board is a "Poetry Center," where students hang up their favorite poems and talk about why those poems were chosen. Throughout the room are different tables used as learning centers, or, as Stephanie refers to them, "hubs," places filled with artifacts students bring in to share, places where students gather to focus on particular interests—science, social studies, art, math—and work together to deepen their knowledge.

One of these hubs is for research writing. Students bring in graphs, timelines, and other charts from the newspaper; in fact, newspaper clippings in general become an important vehicle to learn about what's happening in the community and act as a catalyst to bring about meaningful conversation. The class talks about what they think the items mean, and they begin to interpret the data. They learn from their research and they write and they learn some more in ways that are interesting and make sense to them.

Evaluation

Besides the evaluating Stephanie might do when she responds to student work, she and the students keep portfolios of their writing. She believes that students are the ones who need to be aware of the best examples of breadth and depth in their work, and for this reason the students are the ones who choose the pieces they want in their portfolios as examples. They then write up a brief statement saying what the pieces show about their thinking and their writing. An example of breadth would be a child writing in different genres—mysteries, tall tales, nonfiction, and humor, for example—and Stephanie will introduce her students to authors who write in these various genres to help the children become familiar with them. Regarding depth, the portfolio might show different drafts of one piece, with a student's comments about what he or she learned each time the piece was revisited, the different levels of thinking and insight that occurred.

As for the writing itself, Stephanie believed firmly in learning from the various processes professional writers go through. Who better to learn from? Learning must be authentic to engage children—after all, they'll be learners for their entire lives, and one of a teacher's responsibilities is to help prepare them for the world they encounter every day—and Stephanie had seen students accomplish amazingly sophisticated pieces when treated as real writers themselves. This would be no different in a multiage classroom, except that the older children would be able to help the younger children reach even further than they might have in a same-age grouping situation. Younger children are much more likely to learn from and copy the behaviors of older peers than of adults.

The process, which includes various stages—prewriting (brainstorming ideas), drafting (getting ideas down on paper), revising (finding out what the piece is trying to say, and rewriting accordingly), editing/proofreading (checking spelling and mechanics), and publishing (writing the final copy of a piece on $8^1/_2 \times 11$-inch paper in a bound-blank or self-constructed book)—is not linear by any means. For example, some writers cannot brainstorm ideas until they've written a draft one or two times already—and not every stage works for every child (some never brainstorm at all). Some children will come back to the same stage over and over again, and some do indeed proceed step by step. What's important is that the tools children need be made available to them when they need them, and of course that the teacher be aware and flexible, able to accommodate individual learning styles.

Students employ a wide range of strategies as they write and use different writing process elements appropriately to communicate with different audiences for a variety of purposes.

The Process in Action

Because story is most often used to construct our lives and make sense of the world, and because young students are, for the most part, familiar with story, Stephanie tends to concentrate on narrative writing in the beginning of the year. Let's follow her and her students through a minilesson.

Prewriting/Brainstorming

Stephanie and her students gather in the writing circle so that they can feel at ease and engaged in conversation. She opens a book that she knows the older children are familiar with and like, and that the younger children, even if they are not already familiar with it, will also be able to grasp. For instance, *Zeke Pippin*, by William Steig, is a favorite of many children in Stephanie's class. She begins to read this story, about a pig who learns to play the harmonica—only every time he plays it, his family falls asleep! He leaves home in a huff, has some revelations while he floats on a raft, heads back home, encounters a nasty group of dogs who want to finish him off, manages to save himself through the use of his intelligence and the harmonica, and learns to use his talent to great benefit. When the book is finished, Stephanie asks, "What happened in that story?"

"That pig got in *some* trouble," Chester, one of the older students, says. "He almost got . . ." (Chester moves a finger across his throat and makes a slicing noise, then rolls on the floor.)

"Yeah," Takiya, another older student, says, "I had to hold my breath!"

"He sure did," Stephanie says. "What do we call that part of a story when the character gets in trouble?"

"What's a carrot . . . a charac . . . what's that word?" asks eight-year-old Yvonne.

"Can someone help Yvonne?" Stephanie asks.

"It's a character," Raul says. "You know, someone in the story."

"The pig!" Chester says. "Zeke!"

"And what do we call it when Zeke gets in trouble?" Stephanie asks.

Students read a wide range of literature from many periods in many genres to build an understanding of the many dimensions (e.g., philosophical, ethical, aesthetic) of human experience.

Students apply a wide range of strategies to comprehend, interpret, evaluate, and appreciate texts. They draw on their prior experience, their interactions with other readers and writers, their knowledge of word meaning and other texts, their word identification strategies, and their understanding of textual features (e.g., sound-letter correspondence, sentence structure, context, graphics).

Students participate as knowledgeable, reflective, creative, and critical members of a variety of literacy communities.

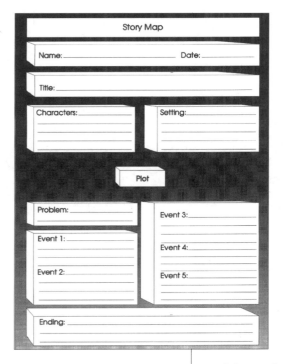

Story Map

Name: _____ Date: _____

Title: _____

Characters: _____   Setting: _____

Plot

Problem: _____   Event 3: _____

Event 1: _____   Event 4: _____

Event 2: _____   Event 5: _____

Ending: _____

Students employ a wide range of strategies as they write and use different writing process elements appropriately to communicate with different audiences for a variety of purposes.

"The problem?" Takiya says.

"The problem," Stephanie says, "or we might also call it the conflict. There was a problem for Zeke in the story when those dogs tied him up, wasn't there?"

The discussion continues. Along with conflict and character, the class talks about other story elements like setting ("Where did that story happen?"), resolutions ("What did Zeke do to get out of his problem?"), and endings ("How did things work out at the end of the story? What was different from the beginning?").

Stephanie then illustrates how the students can use those elements in their own stories by talking about the similarities between what some students have written and what happens in *Zeke Pippin*: "Marcus wrote about the time his little brother wet the bed and cried when his mother found out. That's an example of a problem in a story too. And what happened at the end of your story, Marcus?"

"My mama said she wet the bed when she was little too," Marcus replies.

"And your brother felt better after that?"

"Yeah," Marcus says.

"So things changed in your story, just as things changed for Zeke."

Marcus looks as if he's going to blow up with pride. "Uh huh," he says.

"See? We can all write stories," Stephanie says. "We have so many stories to tell that you can't even count them all!"

The students keep notebooks that they call their reading logs. In these logs are ideas for stories, problems the children encounter as they write, discoveries they make when revising, and the many drawings the children sketch out to help tell their stories more clearly. Stephanie asks the children to read from their lists of ideas to get the discussion about their own work going and to help the students become interested in writing something new. She then demonstrates some strategies the children can use, such as filling in a story map, using a web on draft paper, and drawing what the story might be. Some of the younger children are still making the transition from drawing to writing, and this also helps the visual learners in the class make the connection between pictures and words.

A strategy Stephanie has found to be successful with children of different ages is to use a "galley sheet" to block out story. A student folds an eleven-by-seventeen-inch piece of paper to create thirty-two squares (sixteen on the front and sixteen on the back). Each block of space represents one page in a "blank book" of about the number of pages in a children's literature book. The students use the following format, based on the real books they read, to help them begin to number pages:

First blank page	i	Title page (demonstrated during each read-aloud)
Second blank page	ii	Copyright page
Third blank page	iii	Dedication page
Fourth blank page	1	Page one of story, etc.

The galley sheet format allows students to see the "whole" story. Because children are usually familiar with picture books, it's natural for them to write their own books in that form. The galley sheet gives both older and younger students the opportunity to combine visual and verbal skills to tell their stories in ways meaningful to them, as well as to become aware of how books are put together, in a way that isn't overwhelming. Because of the multiage grouping, young students (who at this age often want very much to appear "grown-up" like the big kids) learn that picture books are not considered "baby" material, and the older students have the opportunity to show their expertise, which instills in them a sense of pride and accomplishment rather than embarrassment at reading and writing in this format. Stephanie also makes sure she has an ample supply of picture books of varying complexity to serve as models for the students' writing. The younger students may be more comfortable with the simpler texts, but the older students want and need more challenging material. No matter what part of the reading and writing continuum they're on, the students are able to choose books that speak to them, and it is also useful for this group, who are at a stage of development at which they

are concerned with doing things "right" because they're aware of audience in a way they hadn't been earlier (Gardner 1980), to see all around them books written in many different ways, all of them "right." In front of them are those squares of pages to fill, and they feel more confident about telling their own stories in their own ways. They are authors and their galley sheets are calling.

Revision

Sometimes students tend to think of revision as cleaning up their crafts—tying up word choice, inserting punctuation—but to revise means to "re-see." Stephanie concentrates on meaning with her students, and because what a story is about can be lost if the writer focuses prematurely on editing, she encourages students to think about the "three R's" of revision: Reread, Rethink, and Rewrite. Helpful ways for students to understand the concept of revision are through conferring in different ways—either with the entire class, with peers, with the teacher, or alone.

Whole-Group Conferences
Stephanie demonstrates a whole-group conference first, since the students need to learn how to talk about story. She asks students to listen carefully, because she needs their help in making the draft better, and reads a piece of her own writing from the "author's chair." Then she asks questions like the following:

- What do you think this story is about?
- What is your favorite part of the story? Why?
- What didn't you understand?
- How did the story make you feel?
- Are there places you wanted something else to happen? Where are they? Why did you want something different there?

- Where can I put in more description?
- Where does my character need to think on the page?
- Where do I need more detail?

Of course, if there are elements in the story to discuss (such as dialogue, internal thoughts, and conflict), this is an opportune time for the students to learn about them from Stephanie's demonstration. She's careful to point out what she wants the students to learn by saying things like, "These are the kinds of questions you need to ask each other when you read your own writing. Now, let's think about how we might answer." This is an important step. Many students tend to want to say simply, "I like it," or "I didn't like it," and leave it at that. But Stephanie stresses that as writers, they must help one another become better at what they do. By helping Stephanie figure out what strategies she might undertake for her own work, the students become empowered to work with each other as the experts.

Peer Conferences

A student may read a story to a classmate, who listens carefully. At the story's conclusion, the writer asks questions like the ones Stephanie has demonstrated in the whole-group conference. Acting as one another's readers helps both classmates to become more thoughtful and attentive readers. In learning to respond to the writing of others they are also acquiring strategies for use in their own reading and writing.

Teacher Conferences

Stephanie tends to underplay this type of conference, because it's important that the students learn to rely on one another and not just on her—otherwise she'd probably wear herself out running from desk to desk trying to read students' work and talk with them about it! A delicate balance needs to be created, and it's up to her to create it; she's very much aware of her presence as the adult authority in the room, but she knows that if the students start to write for her approval, they'll be limiting themselves and become afraid to take the risks that are important for writers to take in order to develop. And yet she also knows that "conferring is at the heart of the writing workshop" (Calkins 1994, 223), and that unless she shows the students what an effective one-on-one conference looks like she can't expect them to confer with one another. She needs to know every student as well—who they are as writers, what they need from her—in order to best help them get on their way. Therefore, many of her questions are not quite the same as the ones in the whole-group or peer conferences. As Lucy Calkins states, there is a "research" phase of conferring that teachers need to be aware of when getting to know their students and their writing. She illustrates the questions that might be asked:

- Can you tell me about how you wrote this?
- How's it going?
- What problems have you [had] while writing this?
- When you read over your [story], how do you feel about it?
- If you were to lay out all your finished drafts and then sort them into piles of "very best," "good," and "less good," which pile would this be in? Why?
- What are you planning to do next? If you *were* going to do more with this piece, what might you do?

- What kind of writing are you trying to do? Do you have a sense of how you want your writing to be in the end?
- How long have you been working on this draft? (1994, 226)

These kinds of questions provide Stephanie and the writer both with different kinds of information. Stephanie learns about the student's writing process and notes how she might best help that student. The student learns how to become a critic of his or her own work without having to rely on Stephanie. After all, she won't be by their sides for the rest of their writing lives!

Self Conferences

After learning about what kinds of questions to ask one another, students work with Stephanie to come up with their own set of criteria that they can use when they choose to work alone. They work as a group to come up with a list of questions, and then put this list into their own writing folders. Here's an example of the criteria one class established:

- How does it sound?
- What is the most important part? Am I telling it clearly?
- Should I change or add words to make that part more clear?
- What part do I like best? Should I explain more about it?
- How else could I write this? Should I try another way?
- What questions might readers ask about this piece? What might they think?
- How can I make readers have a feeling (sad, happy, excited, scared, worried) when they read this piece? What feeling do I want them to have?
- What am I going to do next? (Rewrite, confer with someone, edit, keep on writing, revise, finish draft.)

Students employ a wide range of strategies as they write and use different writing process elements appropriately to communicate with different audiences for a variety of purposes.

Students use spoken, written, and visual language to accomplish their own purposes (e.g., for learning, enjoyment, persuasion, and the exchange of information).

For eight- and nine-year-old students, revision tends to mean starting an entirely new piece or making little corrections to what's already on the page. For ten-year-olds, a consciousness about their process begins to emerge, and, as Lucy Calkins points out, they "can develop [an] ability to coach, admonish, and advise themselves as they write" (1994, 149). Here is an opportunity for Stephanie to encourage the older children to demonstrate revising for the younger. How much more coherent and sophisticated they become when they see the power of their reflection! It encourages them to become astute thinkers, to open up the world for themselves and one another. They're able to plan their writing out loud beside the younger children ("In this piece I want to stretch out the part where Jamie wanted to hit me and what I did about it because it was a big part of the story"), which allows the younger children to think in ways they might not have otherwise. Stephanie also offers careful support to the older children, because on the other side of their newly found awareness is a tendency to block themselves if they become too self-critical. This is where the younger children also come in—they still exhibit carefree, uninhibited ways of seeing and writing, and whenever possible Stephanie points out how the children can learn from one another's strengths. Everyone benefits. Everyone learns.

Editing/Proofreading

Even though Stephanie feels that students must initially concentrate on their meaning when they write, there does come the time when mechanics are important so that other readers can understand that meaning. Stephanie observes the children's writing and keeps a log of what she sees. For instance, she might notice that quite a few are having trouble with putting in periods or with spelling certain words. Here is an opportunity for her to hold a minilesson that is relevant to the children rather than teaching skills out of context. This is how the lesson might go:

Stephanie says, "I've noticed that some of us are spelling words different ways. Here are some of the words," and she writes the various versions on the blackboard:

Becuse	Becz	Because
Thay	They	Da
Wate	Wait	Wet
Reading	Rdng	Reding
Peepul	Pepol	People
Picture	Picshur	Pixshr

"Isn't it something how many different ways we think a word might be spelled?" she asks. What's important to Stephanie at this point is that the children feel pride in taking a risk in their spelling rather than embarrassment at not having done it "the right way." "You know, you are pretty clever thinkers to come up with all these! I am really proud that you're not afraid to try out new words or hard words that you want to use. Let's think about some ways we can learn what these words look like."

They talk about how certain words "just look right," and how certain letters when put together make certain sounds. Stephanie points out, for instance, that Jarrod, an eight-year-old, wrote "da" for "they," because that's how it sounded to him. (Jarrod pronounces "they" as "day.") She gives him credit for being very smart to figure that out, because Jarrod and the other students need to know that they already have a lot of knowledge that will help them. Then she says, "Let's see what the word *they* looks like," and she circles the correct version on the board. "If anybody had trouble spelling *they*, please write it down for yourselves so you can look at it next time," she says. This way, the students create their own individualized spelling lists in a way that makes sense to them, and in a way that applies to their own writing. Later, Stephanie will confer with individual students to give them further one-on-one support for their writing as a whole. As Sandra Wilde (1992) states, "What children with problems in spelling need first is to work on building confidence. Second, such children can participate in the same kinds of curriculum that are helpful for all children, supplemented by additional one-on-one work with the teacher. Reverting to isolated skill-and-drill exercises can end up making things worse. It makes spelling boring and isolates it from writing, and also reinforces a sense of stigma in the child" (152).

Stephanie also has the children write about what they're learning as spellers once a week. This helps them to become aware of their spelling knowledge and gives her a record of their growth. Whether they are "knowing more new words, easily getting more words right in first drafts, coming up with better spellings of hard words, proofreading [or] using resources more effectively. . . . [t]he children themselves are the best judge of where they've been, where they are, and where they need to go" (Wilde, 151).

Stephanie also has students pick out words they want to know how to spell—a list of five words per week that they become aware of through their reading and writing—rather than using spelling textbooks. In many cases, the spelling textbooks's list of words are already familiar to some children and are therefore not an effective learning tool. When students develop their own lists, however, their learning is more relevant to them and more helpful.

When students write words like "da" for "they," they are writing what is known as invented spelling. Because Stephanie pointed out to Jarrod the logic of "da" and showed him how to reach beyond what he had attempted on his own, the chances are that he'll learn the correct spelling of *they* much more effectively than if Stephanie had simply shown him without giving him credit for his efforts. The next time, he'll try an even more sophisticated strategy because it was safe for him to take the first risk, and Stephanie will again help create a bridge for his knowledge in a way that will be useful to him. And so it goes. And so it should: how much better for children to learn to like spelling and be engaged with it than to think of it as boring and of themselves as "dumb" because they "can't" spell!

The same goes for punctuation, which can be very enjoyable if approached that way. Sandra Wilde points out that "learning to punctuate is developmental; children's hypotheses about punctuation grow out of their experience with written language and evolve over time" (119). Again, Stephanie points out effective use of punctuation during read-aloud time with the children's favorite books, and if she notices a student using punctuation in an effective way in his or her writing she points that out to the class. Students will often "overuse" the newly learned marks initially, but that's a natural way of becoming familiar with them. Think of the thousands of exclamation marks written on a page when their purpose first becomes known to a child. Eventually, the overuse will be toned down, but while a child is experimenting, it's important to allow some extra room for exploration.

Children's innate and learned knowledge of punctuation varies, and Stephanie uses a curriculum chart conceived of by Sandra Wilde to help her think about the different levels of sophistication and strategies:

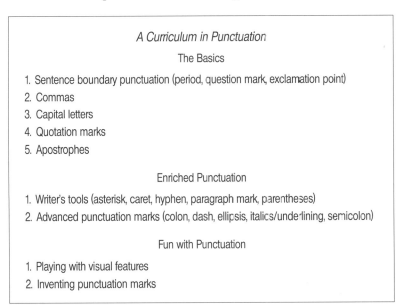

A Curriculum in Punctuation

The Basics

1. Sentence boundary punctuation (period, question mark, exclamation point)
2. Commas
3. Capital letters
4. Quotation marks
5. Apostrophes

Enriched Punctuation

1. Writer's tools (asterisk, caret, hyphen, paragraph mark, parentheses)
2. Advanced punctuation marks (colon, dash, ellipsis, italics/underlining, semicolon)

Fun with Punctuation

1. Playing with visual features
2. Inventing punctuation marks

The chart helps Stephanie keep track of what her students need to learn throughout the year. She keeps records of their growth, and always waits for the "teachable moment"–those points when a teacher knows by a child's question or observation that he or she is ready to learn something new.

If students have difficulty with certain concepts in their writing, Stephanie sits with them one-on-one to help support them. She might read their pieces out loud to them; this is an effective way to illustrate the use of the comma or period, which many children seem to forget as they rush ahead with their thoughts on the page. "Where do you think I should have stopped?" Stephanie will ask, and she'll read the piece again, so the student can tell her where pauses need to occur. "Good. Mark that on the page for you and the reader," Stephanie says, because, after all, punctuation is a tool we use in order to make the reader's job easier. "It's a favor we do for readers," Stephanie often says. "It's how we're polite on the page." Another strategy is to rewrite a student's piece with words correctly spelled and sentences punctuated (respecting ownership, Stephanie does not correct over the student's writing but types or writes a new version), then to sit with students and have them compare the two. That way they learn to figure things out for themselves, based on the meaning they have created. Or the teacher can take a passage from a favorite author and distribute copies to the students, typed with no punctuation. Students sit in small groups and punctuate the passage themselves, and then compare what they've done to the author's punctuated version.

There is a chart in the writing hub that students add to throughout the year. Each time someone uses punctuation in an effective way, Stephanie asks that student to write it on the chart, along with an explanation of how the mark is used. That way, all the students can refer to the chart for their own purposes, and all can learn in their own ways. Often the children will also discuss punctuation they notice in their reading of published works.

It's important to point out that Stephanie keeps the spelling and punctuation lessons as brief as possible so the children don't become overwhelmed or bored. The lessons are always meaningful within the context of the students' own writing or the writing of authors they enjoy–never in isolation.

Because the children learn about conventions of language as related to their writing, and because Stephanie points out the way students intuitively use language correctly, they learn to actually *like* punctuation and spelling and therefore use it effectively. How different this is from endlessly filling out worksheets and then forgetting the rules they're supposed to inculcate because there's no context to put those rules into! Stephanie learned from the example of Mary Ellen Giacobbe, who has been written about by researchers such as Donald Graves and Lucy Calkins. Giacobbe recognizes the achievements of students who use good language conventions and keeps a list of those achievements for all students to refer to when they do their own editing. This way, students have their peers to refer to as real-life role models, something especially important in a multiage classroom. Therefore, when Stephanie confers with the students about their writing, she is careful to point out to each one where he or she has done something that others can learn from, and makes up an editing checklist based on those examples. Students keep the lists in their writing folders, refer to them, and add what they have learned so they can in turn share that knowledge with those they confer with. In this way, they take pride in their accomplishments, and grammar becomes a good learning experience. Here are some examples that Stephanie's students have come up with:

Students apply knowledge of language structure, language conventions (e.g., spelling and punctuation), media techniques, figurative language, and genre to create, critique, and discuss print and nonprint texts.

Students participate as knowledgeable, reflective, creative, and critical members of a variety of literacy communities.

- Do I start my sentences with capital letters?
- Do I need to use the dictionary to find words I'm not sure about spelling?
- Do my sentences end where they should? If not, do I need to put periods in?
- Where do I need to take a breath in the sentence? Do I put a comma there?
- When my characters talk, are there quotation marks at the beginning and end of what they say?
- If there's an exciting place in the story, do I use an exclamation mark?
- When I ask questions, do I use a question mark?

To demonstrate editing further, Stephanie also works with the whole class. She asks a volunteer to write a sentence from his or her story on the overhead projector, and then, together, the class helps that student edit. Other strategies include editing with a friend and editing with the teacher.

Students then proofread individually, but Stephanie takes things one step further. As she points out to the class, professional writers often ask others to proofread for them, because it's hard to get everything right sometimes when we work so much on what we want to say. So she asks the students to break into pairs and read each other's work. Sometimes work is read aloud; sometimes it's read in silence and then commented on. In this way, students have the opportunity to help each other and to sharpen their own editing skills—we all become better at our own writing when we read others' carefully and are able to articulate why something might read a certain way. As Stephanie often reminds the students, "We talk to each other about our writing because we care about it."

Pieces are finished when the students feel that their stories are absolutely the best they can be. Now they are ready for publication.

Publishing

Students have a choice about how they want their final pieces to appear. Stories can be written

- in a blank book,
- on 8½-by-11-inch lined paper, or
- in a handmade book, for which the student chooses the format.

Publishing student work sends a very clear message to the children and their parents that writing is valued and is meant to say something to other people. Students learn the concept of audience, and when they know that others are going to be reading their work they are much more likely to want to make it as strong as possible. Publishing also encourages self-esteem in children—their books and what they have to say are valued, and they learn that writing is a strong method of communicating indeed. They also become more aware of how books are put together, which adds insight to their reading processes. Their literacy is enhanced in a way that helps them in the world.

A Student-Generated Step: Acting Out Stories

Since students spontaneously began to act out their stories for one another after they were published (it started with one group of boys "goofing around"), Stephanie decided to incorporate drama and story as part of the writing curriculum. Soon, even the shy students asked others to act out their stories for them. Time was set aside once a week to allow students to perform their stories, and the students began to revise more richly as they heard feedback from their audience of peers. As each group performed a story, members of the class wrote down their favorite parts or favorite lines and even drew pictures of how they would have a character look. Student authors could then take the feedback and make further revision. To keep the process organized and to create a routine the students could rely upon, Stephanie asked for volunteers to write up a sign-up sheet. Those students who wanted to act out fellow students' narratives put their names on the sheet, and the following occurred:

- The student organized a group to act out the story.
- Performances were held three times per week, and each lasted approximately fifteen minutes.
- After the performance, students wrote reflections about it in their daybooks and discussed what they had written.

The success of this strategy made Stephanie think more about presenting opportunities that would support different learning styles so that all students could improve their writing. If she had limited the class's writing experience to writing a rough draft using only lined paper, possibilities would have been limited for many children. Therefore, she writes a list of reflective questions in her journal that she plans to research:

- Would acting out a story with a friend be a prewriting step as well?
- Should students act out events when "stuck" in story?
- What kind of an impact would drama have on students' writing processes?
- How can drama bring out the kinesthetic learner in writing stories?
- For students who are auditory learners, would drafting stories on cassette tape serve as a galley stage better than galley sheets do?
- What about kinesthetic learners? What can stimulate these students' imaginations to develop characters, setting, story events?
- Could music be used to create mood in composing a story?
- Besides acting out final stories, could students use movement to develop events?

Students adjust their use of spoken, written, and visual language (e.g., conventions, style, vocabulary) to communicate effectively with a variety of audiences and for different purposes.

Different Genres

Of course story is not the only way to communicate in writing, and Stephanie works with the children to help them understand the many different ways there are. One strategy she has found to be particularly successful involves letter writing.

The strategy came about when Stephanie was approached by her colleague Maureen Johnson, a drama teacher at Lake Ridge Academy in North Ridgeville, Ohio, about a project called "Write Friends." Maureen teaches a student theater group that works with young authors to bring words to life on stage, and she and Stephanie agreed that the students in Stephanie's class would probably benefit a great deal from the experience. Before a decision was made, however, Stephanie asked the students for their input; after all, they were the ones who would be invested in the project. Stephanie first showed the students a videotape of past troupes in action. She knew that she needed to give students a concrete idea of what the story dramatizations might look like, as well as to give them the "big picture." She believes firmly in this important concept—that older students reading to younger ones, for example, or showing the previous year's projects to the current class, can suggest possibilities and provide clear criteria, which are very important when working with children of different ages. At the end of the tape, Stephanie asked, "Well, what do you think?"

Ben: I liked the music with the stories.

Blair: I liked how they jumped off the stairs and ran across the stage. They flung their arms in the air. They moved around *a lot!*

Danita: I wonder how they made all those noises.

After watching the tape again and talking in more detail about the story, Stephanie and the students agreed that they would like to develop two of their own stories over the next four months for the group to perform. In talking about concerns regarding the performance of the stories, Stephanie and Maureen decided that the first step in developing the creative collaboration was to connect the classrooms at a personal level, to create a level of trust that would enable the students to write freely. Both teachers viewed students' writing as a personal and precious act. To have someone take the stories and perform them on the stage without thought to the creation of a safe and trusting atmosphere between performers and writers would be disastrous.

In order to help this trust develop, Stephanie devised a pen pal activity for the students. She and Maureen first randomly paired the two classrooms' students. Since there were twenty-four elementary and seventeen high school students, some of the high school students had more than one pen pal.

In order to help the students establish meaningful and successful correspondence with the pen pals, Stephanie next guided the children in learning how to write a friendly letter. She began with the project title, "Write Friends."

"What ideas come to mind when you think of this project name?" she asked.

"We wanna be friends," Sam said. "We'll be writing."

Students participate as knowledgeable, reflective, creative, and critical members of a variety of literacy communities.

"What do you do to become friends with someone?"

"I try to like some of the things they like."

"I'm nosy about their family . . . like do they have brothers or sisters and do they get along?"

"I would tell them about my favorite movie."

"OK, I hear some ideas that will help us get started," Stephanie said. "Now, let's do a five-minute freewrite and list things to include in our first letters. Then, we'll move to working groups to develop a list of possible topics we can choose from to include in our letters." She jotted down some of her own ideas, and then circulated around the room, offering encouragement and suggestions.

After the five minutes, the students moved into small groups to share their ideas. Then each group shared theirs with the whole class. The class recorder, a student volunteer, wrote down the ideas on the overhead projector. Following the discussion, the students drafted their letters. If they became "stuck," they could look at the class-generated list of possible topics. Everyone wrote excitedly to his or her pen pal. Stephanie displayed a copy of her draft to Ms. Johnson.

September, 1994

Dear Maureen,

I am looking forward to hearing from you on a regular basis. My students are busy drafting their first letters to their pen pals. We have been talking about what to include in our letters. Since you and I have known each other so long, I do not need to ask you a lot of questions about your likes and needs.

I do want you to know that I am glad that you are my friend and that we will be able to work together on this project. I am optimistic that our collaboration will benefit all of us.

Your "Write Friend,"

Stephanie Sierra
Stephanie Sierra

A student notices that his letter looks different.

"What do you see that's different?" Stephanie asks.

"You have stuff on the top and bottom," the student says.

"What kind of stuff did you notice?" Stephanie asks.

"A date," another student calls out. "There's a date up there."

"That's very observant," Stephanie says. They talk about how the letter has a date, an address, a greeting, a closing, and the letter writer's name. Because the students have brought up what they've noticed about the form, Stephanie takes their lead and helps to point out why letters are written that way. Then she guides them back to the content of the letters themselves. "What do you notice about how I talk to Ms. Johnson in my letter?" she asks.

"You sound like friends," Blair says.

"Yeah, she sounds nice," Chester says.

Stephanie asks the groups to share their letters with one another and find things that are alike. They spend a few moments doing so, and then as each group reports their findings, the recorder again notes the list on a transparency:

- We had questions about pets.
- We had questions about their families.
- Some of the kids told what they looked like.
- Kids told their names and ages.
- What was their favorite TV show? Favorite book?
- Told the pen pal to write back soon.

The students decide to use the letter format to write to their pen pals, since they don't know them very well yet, and since they're excited to show off their newly learned knowledge to the "big high school kids." Again, the focus at this time is on meaning—what the children want to communicate is of the greatest importance, and because they want to communicate, they're able to understand letters as a form in a deeper way than if they were taught the form without having any purpose for it.

Students adjust their use of spoken, written, and visual language (e.g., conventions, style, vocabulary) to communicate effectively with a variety of audiences and for different purposes.

When the children received responses from the high school students (who were as excited about the process as they were), they became even more engaged and sophisticated in their writing. They noticed and made use of some of the ways the high school students wrote, and because they were writing about their stories in order to help their pen pals understand them better for future dramatization, they gained a new way of becoming more aware and thinking about what their stories were actually trying to say.

After several friendly letters from the elementary students, the high school students began to write very informal letters. For example, LuAnn, an eight-year-old student, received a typed letter in all lowercase with the comment, "My shift key is broken." The high school pen pal was sharing a subtle joke, and LuAnn decided to include a joke in her response letter. In another instance, a high school student wrote her letter in the shape of a maze. The younger student then experimented with using different formats—drawings, quotations, shapes, "secret" codes—to share his writing. Because the communication was purposeful and real, students were able to discover ways to play with language and increase their knowledge based on the way the "big kids" wrote.

At the other end, the high school students became interested in dramatizing the students' letters as well as their stories, since they found that the letters lent themselves to deeper interpretations. So, they asked the younger students for permission to use their letters as well. Because of the level of trust between the two groups, the elementary students willingly gave their approval. They trusted their pen pals to respect their work; they had become true writing friends.

When it came time to put on the performance, Maureen, Stephanie, and both groups of students saw the power of their four months of collaboration. The program included the children's names as authors of the stories and letters performed, which validated them as true writers. When they saw their writing—the two stories, along with short essays, family narratives, and their letters—being acted out, they gained an even deeper understanding of how writing reflects real life and makes our experience more meaningful. They saw how they could further their writing. As Maureen Johnson said, "The beauty of this idea is the way it inspires and motivates students to write and revise more to breathe life into their work, because they see clearly from the dramatic interpretation how their words can come alive." This was definitely multiage learning at its best.

As Stephanie and Maureen reflected on this educational event, they found important questions to guide them for future experiences:

- What individual learning occurs for each student?
- How active are the students in determining what happens?
- What curriculum changes may be necessary to improve the level of participation for all students?
- Is the learning process sufficiently public, participatory, and dynamic?

Students use spoken, written, and visual language to accomplish their own purposes (e.g., for learning, enjoyment, persuasion, and the exchange of information).

Both Stephanie and Maureen believe that students need to be given real reasons to develop their creativity and writing fluency, and they value the contributions of partners and learning to work collaboratively in a meaningful way. Because of their awareness of their teaching philosophies, the two were able to work together in guiding students in what turned out to be a truly enlightening and exciting experience for all involved.

The Integrated Curriculum

Another way students experience different genres is through integrated learning. Students use writing so frequently in Stephanie's classroom that it becomes a way to facilitate individual inquiry and enables learners to find connections in what they think and do. For example, Stephanie had submitted a grant proposal to a regional agency for funds to develop a project that integrated entrepreneurship with applied academics in math, science, and the language arts. The students would raise plants to sell, and initially any profits would be used at the discretion of the class. The experience would involve the students in active inquiry—they would define the questions they needed to pursue, research what resources were available to help answer them, and use the scientific method (observing, classifying, predicting, and inferring) to come to know the growing cycle of plants and the conditions that affect their growth.

Science and Language Arts

Using pictures on the seed packets, students first sorted their chosen seeds by the size, colors, and shapes of flowers, and the number of petals. They then used spiral-bound notebooks as science logs to keep records of their observations. Entries consisted of dates and students' findings by classification. Predictions were made about which flowers would bloom and when. As time passed, students used rulers and measuring tapes to record plant height and drew pictures of what they saw. Whenever a plant changed, class discussions were held about what factors might have caused the change. If a student's plant died, the student was given more soil and seeds in order to try again. All the while, the science logs were scrupulously kept up to date.

The first crop of plants flourished until they were transplanted, at which point they all died. Students speculated that the plants might have been too young to transplant, so they started new plants in bigger pots and tried different soil. They wrote their observations in their logs, and, after reading previous notes, discovered that the combination of the soil and the size of the pot, as well as the amount of water and sunlight, affected the plants' growth. They asked their parents and others in their families what might help the plants grow faster, and in this way discovered the use of fertilizer.

Economics and Language Arts

Students also learned about creating and marketing products. One of the questions they decided to pursue was what kinds of products are advertised, how images and drawings enhance advertisements, and what words are used to entice consumers, all of which they researched in newspapers. Because the students intended to sell the plants they'd grown, their inquiry was focused and their learning was connected, relevant, authentic, and directly applicable.

Small groups next worked to come up with a name for their plant business. The class voted on "Flower Power," and decorated brown paper bags to place their products in when the plants were ready to sell. The groups also designed posters and flyers to display in the lunchroom and hallways, and organized schedules for taking turns to stay after school to sell the merchandise. Two students wrote a letter to the principal asking for permission both to run their business and to advertise in the school, and another composed a permission letter for parents to sign so that students could stay after school. Once the permission slips were turned in, Stephanie gave them to the student in charge of the schedule, who would plan which students would stay when. The schedule was then placed in front of the room so that everyone could have the information.

Stephanie learned that asking each student to be responsible for two or more plants made a difference. Since everyone had more than one flowerpot with his or her name on it, no one felt threatened if one plant wouldn't grow—in every case, the other plant did. This ensured that each student would have a plant about which to conduct observations, predictions, and measurements, and, if both plants grew, students had the opportunity to compare them for size, shape, and growth. An added benefit was that the class ended up having more than enough plants to sell in order to make the sale worthwhile.

The students enjoyed the project tremendously. Stephanie noted in her journal that they became truly engaged in academic inquiry as well as the business venture, and they learned about the environment in a way that made the issues real to them. For example, because the class couldn't afford all the new containers they needed, they had to think about other things they could use to grow their plants in. Recycled containers such as milk cartons, clear plastic florist boxes, jars with lids (which acted as greenhouses), and even egg cartons were used, and this allowed the students to see the importance of being able to use things more than once rather than throwing them out without a second thought. Stephanie hadn't realized initially that the necessity for containers could encourage such creativity, problem solving, and critical thinking, but it was the students themselves who came up with the idea of saving used items from their own households and bringing them in for their

Students conduct research on issues and interests by generating ideas and questions, and by posing problems. They gather, evaluate, and synthesize data from a variety of sources (e.g., print and nonprint texts, artifacts, people) to communicate their discoveries in ways that suit their purpose and audience.

project. This revelation made her think of the importance of genuine inquiry, of posing real problems for real solutions, in order to make learning meaningful.

Stephanie saw how the wonders of science and poetry can become easily integrated as well. Students were so taken by some of the flower names (forget-me-nots, zinnias, marigolds, and morning glories, for example) and the pictures of the flowers themselves that they chose to write poems about them. The flowers evoked colorful, innovative images, patterns, and rhythms in the children's language, and Stephanie became more firmly convinced of the way the natural world inspires creativity in all of us.

When the week of the sale arrived, there were sixty-five plants to sell during the last four days of April. A team was organized for each sale day—two students acted as cashiers, two students bagged the plants in the Flower Power bags, and two students acted as hosts for the customers. Twelve to fifteen customers per day came in to purchase the plants; all the plants were sold, and the class collected $52.56, which excited them greatly!

Social Responsibility

Since the Oklahoma City bombing had taken place during this time, and since the students were profoundly affected by the devastation and wanted to do something for the victims' families, they unanimously agreed to donate their profits. They wrote letters to the Oklahoma Red Cross, and Stephanie wrote a check for the entire amount. One student stated in a reflection entry in her science log, "It doesn't matter how old you are, you can always help someone in your own way."

This powerful entry led Stephanie to think about what she could do in the future to help make the experience even richer for the children. Following are some of the thoughts from her journal:

- Would research and creative writing work together to make children more aware, more able to think critically and in new ways about their world?
- What other projects could be used to integrate the curriculum?
- What other community needs could be met?
- Could a curriculum be implemented to address social concerns?
- What could the younger and middle students do the following year to carry this project further?

Moving Ahead

The culture in Stephanie's multiage class demonstrates the importance of participation and student engagement in creating a successful classroom community. She learned that it's essential in the first few weeks of school for her to show and make children aware of the dignity and respect for one another that she expects them to demonstrate throughout the year. Although the first year involved a great deal of work and wondering, it also made Stephanie realize that students can learn and demonstrate their knowledge in ways not even imagined possible if only they're given the right conditions and the room they need in order to learn. The following year will be exciting in its own right, because brand-new students will be welcomed by the students who will be in Stephanie's class for another year or two. The older students help ease the beginning-of-school anxieties the younger students may have, and the new students see for themselves that it is indeed possible to like coming back to your teacher and your classroom. The older students will demonstrate how things operate, and, to provide an opportunity for the newcomers to feel a real ownership, Stephanie will hold an opening discussion to revisit the way things were done the previous year in order for the community to determine whether some things will be handled differently. It should be noted that this happens throughout the year as well—if some things don't work, the class discusses why and they come up with possible alternative strategies. The younger students in the class are supported in their participation, and, although there will be a few slips, the older students will demonstrate effective class discussion behavior. Students quickly learn that they are welcome and that their input is critical to everyone's learning experience.

Imagine that you are Stephanie and that this is *your* experience. It's the end of the year now, and even though you may feel that you've put in more work, and that there have been moments more difficult, than you ever thought possible given all your years of teaching, you know something profound has happened. You feel more energetic about the work you do, because you see students wanting to learn, and you see how most of them have exceeded the expectations of every adult around them. You find that parents have become your allies and strong advocates for the work you do. Even achievement scores have gone up, much to everyone's delight. You've exceeded your own expectations professionally, and you're no longer afraid of learning new ways to teach and learn. Your colleagues have participated in the learning as well, and the administration has taken notice.

This is how it begins.

What Key Standards Emerge in This Chapter?

Students employ a wide range of strategies as they write and use different writing process elements appropriately to communicate with different audiences for a variety of purposes.

Stephanie helps her students by asking them questions to lead them to think more deeply about their writing, or to help them get "unstuck." She models constructive criticism to help students see their strengths and in turn help themselves and one another become more sophisticated about their work. She also guides the children to read their work aloud to her or to one another to hear what they might miss by sight reading alone. Whatever the strategy, Stephanie makes it clear to her students that she is invested in what they want to communicate.

Students read a wide range of print and nonprint texts to build understanding of texts, themselves, and the cultures of the United States and the world. Among these texts are fiction and nonfiction, classic and contemporary works.

Stephanie knows that writing and reading are so closely entwined that the two cannot truly be thought of as separate entities. Therefore, she supports her students by making sure the classroom is filled with books of all different kinds and genres, as well as by asking them to bring in newspaper clippings of events in the community, country, and world to share. The students are encouraged to discuss what they learn with one another—there's even a special place in the classroom devoted to such discussion.

Students apply a wide range of strategies to comprehend, interpret, evaluate, and appreciate texts. They draw on their prior experience, their interactions with other readers and writers, their knowledge of word meaning and other texts, their word identification strategies, and their understanding of textual features (e.g., sound-letter correspondence, sentence structure, context, graphics).

The literature discussion that Stephanie has with the class while reading *Zeke Pippin* illustrates how important it is for students to relate literature to their lives, and how sophisticated their understanding of text can be when allowed and encouraged to do so. Yvonne, for instance, struggles with both the word *character* and its concept. Had she been in an environment where she didn't feel comfortable thinking in her own way and asking questions to clarify, she might have kept silent, not understanding the discussion around her, and risked becoming overwhelmed and lost in her learning. When conflict is discussed, Stephanie asks Marcus to share the story of his brother's bedwetting. She points out how Marcus grasped the concept of conflict in his own writing, and Marcus learns that he's a skilled and competent writer. The other children learn that they too, have what it takes to become writers.

Students participate as knowledgeable, reflective, creative, and critical members of a variety of literacy communities.

By talking about Zeke Pippin, the students learn how to critique literature through discussion of story elements. By keeping their reading logs, they learn to reflect on and critique their own and one another's material. They come up with their own lists of questions/criteria to ask themselves in order to make their writing better. They act out their stories in partnership with high school students. They write letters to communicate. And, they even become sophisticated enough to combine creative writing (in this case, poetry) with research writing in their science plant project.

Students use spoken, written, and visual language to accomplish their own purposes (e.g., for learning, enjoyment, persuasion, and the exchange of information).

The various kinds of talk, writing, reading, and drawing in this chapter show the wealth of ways in which the children in Stephanie's class learn in all kinds of contexts. In communicating with one another, with their high school pen pals, and with the community at large, both locally and in Oklahoma City, they are defining and pursuing their own goals.

Students apply knowledge of language structure, language conventions (e.g., spelling and punctuation), media techniques, figurative language, and genre to create, critique, and discuss print and nonprint texts.

The positive ways in which Stephanie and the children learn about spelling helps all of them to feel comfortable in taking risks and reaching beyond their current knowledge. The children learn that spelling can actually be fun, and because they're engaged, they become better spellers. Stephanie also becomes a better teacher. She could have, for instance, shrugged off Jarrod's interpretation of the word "they" by spelling it as "da," dismissing it as yet another case of Jarrod not "getting it." Instead, she understands the thinking behind Jarrod's attempts, and she helps him to be aware of different sound and letter combinations in a way that he can utilize to good advantage. The different hubs throughout the classroom—on research writing, poetry, art, math, science, social studies—help children to focus on different genres and subjects and work together to broaden and deepen their knowledge. In the writing hub is a punctuation chart that students write on whenever they use punctuation in a new or effective way; they put the mark on the chart along with an explanation of how and why they used it. Other students refer to the chart for their own purposes, and they learn language conventions not only from Stephanie but from one another in a way that makes sense to them.

References and Resources for Further Reading

Aulgur, L., Baker, L., and Copeland, K. (1992, Spring). Multi-age classrooms: Options to an outdated system. *Teacher's Networking, the Whole Language Newsletter 11* (2), 1, 3.

Bargh, J., and Shul, Y. (1980). On the cognitive benefits of teaching. *Journal of Educational Psychology 72*, 593–604.

Braddock, J. H., II (with J. M. McPartland). (1990, April). Alternatives to tracking. *Educational Leadership, 47* (7), 76–79.

Calkins, L. 1994. *The art of teaching writing* (2nd ed.). Portsmouth, NH: Heinemann.

Chase, P., and Doan, J. (1994). *Full circle: A new look at multiage education.* Portsmouth, NH: Heinemann.

Ellis, S., Rogoff, B., and Cromer, C. (1981). Age segregation in children's social interactions. *Developmental Psychology 17* (4), 399–407.

Gardner, H. (1983). *Frames of mind: The theory of multiple intelligences.* New York: Basic Books.

Glickman, C. (1991, May). Pretending not to know what we know. *Educational Leadership 48* (8), 4–10.

Goodman, K. (1988). *What's whole in whole language?* Portsmouth, NY: Heinemann.

Graves, D. (1994). *A fresh look at writing.* Portsmouth, NH: Heinemann.

Harste, J., Short, K., and Burke, C. (1988). *Creating classrooms for authors.* Portsmouth, NH: Heinemann.

McClellan, D. E. (1994). Multiage grouping: Implications for education. In Chase and Doan (pp. 147–166).

Peterson, R. (1992). *Life in a crowded place: Making a learning community.* Portsmouth, NH: Heinemann.

Routman, R. (1988). *Transitions: From literature to literacy.* Portsmouth, NH: Heinemann.

Routman, R. (1991). *Invitations: Changing as teachers and learners K–12.* Portsmouth, NH: Heinemann.

Slavin, R. E. (1988, September). Synthesis of research on grouping in elementary and secondary schools. *Educational Leadership 46* (1), 67–77.

Slavin, R. E. (1991, March). Are cooperative learning and "untracking" harmful to the gifted? Response to Allan. *Educational Leadership 48* (6), 68–71.

Steig, W. (1994). *Zeke Pippin.* New York: HarperCollins Children's Books.

Tierney, R. (Ed.). (1991). *Portfolio assessment in reading-writing classrooms.* Norwood, MA: Christopher-Gordon.

Wilde, S. (1991). *You kan red this! Spelling and punctuation for whole language classrooms, K–6.* Portsmouth, NH: Heinemann.

CHAPTER FIVE

"... AND JUSTICE FOR ALL"

Anthony rushed to his seat after recess and pulled out his math homework. He had spent hours on the problems; his row had had to complete all the evens, and he had done them all without error. His father had even checked to make sure before he left for his job at the lab.

Mr. Landis called the class to order and walked up and down the rows to make sure the students had done their homework. Finally, he returned to the front of the room and asked for volunteers to do the problems. Anthony's hand shot up—it wouldn't matter which problem he was assigned; he could do them all! Mr. Landis didn't call on Anthony. Instead, he chose students whose hands weren't raised. Simon was one of those students, and he didn't know the answer. He looked at Anthony, pleading in his eyes. Anthony bent over, pretending to tie his shoe, and whispered the answer, which Simon gave to Mr. Landis.

Mr. Landis looked at Anthony, and his words seemed to splinter as he said, "There are a flock of birds on a fence. The farmer counts them and realizes there are 30. He runs into the yard and all but 20 percent fly away. How many birds remain?"

"None," Anthony replied.

"Seems you have only one right answer today, and you gave it to Simon," Mr. Landis said. "You will stay in during recess to complete more problems."

Anthony stared down at his book. He was confused. If he were one of the birds, and they were frightened by the farmer in the yard, he would have left too. It was just like when he and his friends were playing; if they were frightened away from the lot in the alley, they would *all* leave. As for Simon, well, he was Anthony's *compadre*'s (godfather's) son. He could not leave Simon embarrassed in front of the class.

Mr. Landis was wrong. Anthony *did* have many right answers. It was just that Mr. Landis didn't ask the right questions.

Power. For many of us, moving toward a more learner-centered, democratic classroom is about power. The power to determine who is taught, what is taught, and how well it is taught.

If we look at Anthony's situation, we can see clearly what happens to children when teachers aren't aware—whether of power issues or of a student's way of thinking. Instead of trying to understand what Anthony's answer about the birds reveals about his thinking, Mr. Landis responds from a set of assumptions about how all students should interpret a question. He failed to recognize the social nature of constructing meaning, or how the student's values, interests, and experiences shape his or her way of interpreting the world. In addition, Mr. Landis allowed his own self-interest in letting the students know who's in charge increase their perception that they have little or no importance in the classroom.

In a democratic classroom, however, structures are put in place to afford opportunity to *all* students to move from their own life experiences into even wider experiences enriched by diverse ideas, views, and voices. Problem-based learning encourages students to start with loosely structured (or open-ended) questions and engage in complex activities that require them to reflect, probe, and search for answers. Democratic classrooms invite multiple perspectives for discussion to ensure that students hear, read, and think about a wide range of ideas and possibilities. Groups are organized to give students the experience of hearing from others of differing backgrounds and abilities in order to learn to respect others' opinions.

> Students develop an understanding of and respect for diversity in language use, patterns, and dialects across cultures, ethnic groups, geographic regions, and social roles.
>
> Students participate as knowledgeable, reflective, creative, and critical members of a variety of literacy communities.

For me, this story illustrates one catalyst for my own journey of reflection and change. I had not been teaching for very long, but in the urban setting in which I had grown up, students from different cultures were often invisible in public classrooms. When this story was shared with me (and it did actually happen), I was torn. Mr. Landis's insensitivity was indeed devastating to a student from Anthony's culture, because that culture holds teachers in high esteem. To be rejected by a person of such rank was to be rejected deeply; young Anthony's confusion had to do with more than the math problem; it also had to do with the deep values prescribed by his Mexican heritage.

Another episode that had a strong influence on my teaching beliefs took place while I was in college. I had successfully campaigned for a seat on the Student Senate, and when the newly elected senate met to determine the officers, one suggestion was to name the person who had received the most votes as president. This particular suggestion pleased me, since I had received most of the votes. I, however, was not selected, because the suggestion was modified to name the *male* with the greatest number of votes. I was struck by the unfairness of this incident, to which the others seemed blind. Even other female members did not view this tactic as unfair. "It just seems more natural to see a guy as president," I was told. This was quite contrary to the deep structure of values I had formulated; I had graduated from an all-girl high school where females were the decision makers, the leaders, the creators, the participants in the school culture, and yes, even the troublemakers. It was as natural for me to think of a president being female as it was for others to think of a male.

Over the years, this memory nagged at me, kept coming back to me as though it wouldn't be quieted, until I understood that I have a responsibility as the teacher in my classroom to make sure that this same kind of situation doesn't arise with the girls I teach. I try to see that I give girls my complete attention when I answer their questions, since studies have shown that all too often we allow the boys to pull us away from attending to the girls. I try to make sure that I scaffold questions for girls the same way I do for boys. I make sure that everyone has time and quiet to think. When students are in small groups, I will not allow gender to be a reason to determine who has what role. I try to encourage students to see themselves doing things that stretch their abilities, however those abilities have been labeled by themselves or others. Just as many young women I have taught have not envisioned themselves as leaders or as being in charge, they also have not viewed themselves as successful learners. Our school systems have been wonderful in giving them plenty of snapshots of their short-comings and limitations. What we need to do is give students a full-length movie that shows the struggle and, more important, the growth from experience and the possibilities that lie ahead. Students need to see learning as something that continues over a lifetime, not as a start-and-stop freeze-frame.

These were the two experiences I thought of when I began my teaching career, and they helped me to begin to understand the importance of democracy in our schools. And from there, the following initial questions started to guide me, and continue to guide me professionally every day:

- How do I help to create a classroom where every voice and language is heard and valued?
- How can I help students develop confidence as meaning makers who want to share what they know through a variety of ways that will enhance their learning?
- How can I support students who are trying new learning strategies?
- How can I connect learning with the student's sense of here and now?
- How can I provide access to the tools that will help students use what they know to address gaps in existing and new knowledge?

Developing a Classroom That Looks Inviting

Like the other teachers featured in this book, I left my classroom and looked to where students liked to be. They all seemed to enjoy the music room, the gym, the art room, the playground. So I asked them to tell me more; I asked them to let me know what they liked to do away from school. I heard about the after-school drama program, park district programs, and recreational or formal sports. I learned that students like, for example:

- Choosing what they draw in art
- Playing board games with others
- Playing kickball
- Creating music

From these responses and others like them, I learned about students' basic needs for choice, socializing, variety, and success. I then had two new questions to explore:

- How could I structure my classroom to be inviting?
- What could I do to foster continued enthusiasm in learning?

I observed the way in which students' favorite classrooms were organized. For the most part, they were set up to optimize the activities that were to take place: the gym had stations for practice and development; the art room enabled students to spread out so they could leave works in process in safe areas, and it

---

(Sidebar notes, left margin:)

Students develop an understanding of and respect for diversity in language use, patterns, and dialects across cultures, ethnic groups, geographic regions, and social roles.

Students whose first language is not English make use of their first language to develop competency in the English language arts and to develop understanding of content across the curriculum.

Students use spoken, written, and visual language to accomplish their own purposes (e.g., for learning, enjoyment, persuasion, and the exchange of information).

---

had enticing and easily accessible drawing and painting tools in sight; the music area had inviting spaces for solo, ensemble, and whole-group practice. In each area, students were able to move about without disturbing the work of others, they engaged in hands-on learning that applied directly to the subject matter, and they could see others absorbed in the learning process as well. These rooms were reflective of learner-centered principles. In other words, the rooms were set up *for the students*. The atmosphere was welcoming, and the message was that students were encouraged to choose activities of interest where their participation and performance were respected and valued.

These classrooms didn't just "happen." When I talked with my colleagues, I found that each spent a great deal of time listening to students, as well as explaining and reinforcing expectations for how the students would interact. The students knew that if they lost or broke equipment or disturbed the rest of the community, they wouldn't be the only ones to suffer for it. Not only their learning experience, but the experience of others would be compromised and put in jeopardy. These teachers were crystal clear in illustrating and demonstrating responsibility for keeping their learning community at its best, and the students took this responsibility seriously.

I began to picture what I could do to transform my classroom into a room that would support instruction that offered choice, variety, and both individual and group inquiry. Instead of rows, desks would be moved into clusters to facilitate group work. I planned to designate an area of the room as the reading corner, equipped with rug, beanbag chair, and bookcase filled with a variety of good books. As students did independent reading, I would ask them to write blurbs about their books and put them on the Readers' Bulletin Board. This might be a low-risk activity that wasn't required, but it would offer others—especially those having difficulty in choosing books—a good place to start when they searched for titles of interest.

Where might they write? Why not a writing corner?

This room would look inviting. And along with the new look would develop a curriculum, negotiated with the students, that would optimize the resources in their community.

I also participated in a National Endowment for the Humanities seminar entitled "Literature and the Creative Self" at Southern Illinois University, and was introduced to Louise Rosenblatt's work on reader-response theory. It made sense to me that a student's response be valued as part of interaction with text; my quest for ideas to help students realize that their meanings counted might start here.

I learned from the seminar to look at drama and art as ways to "enter" or respond to text; I learned about developing Independent Learning Packets, which might consist of a number of different articles on a topic, a video, probes for possible explorations, or audiotapes—anything that might help a student relate to the text in a more meaningful way. And, I learned more about structuring groups, which excited me because I believed strongly from my experience that working in groups helped students get along better and learn to appreciate and value their differences while seeing their commonalities. Previously, I had been discouraged from having students work in groups, because they "might

— Students read a wide range of print and nonprint texts to build an understanding of texts, of themselves, and of the cultures of the United States and the world; to acquire new information; to respond to the needs and demands of society and the workplace; and for personal fulfillment. Among these texts are fiction and nonfiction, classic and contemporary works.

— Students use a variety of technological and informational resources (e.g., libraries, databases, computer networks, video) to gather and synthesize information and to create and communicate knowledge.

cheat on reading skill sheets." Yet now I had the information I needed, and I would follow my professional instincts in order to be a better teacher. The other kind of teaching—the kind with the skill sheets and the mistrust and the testing of children for what they don't know rather than what they do—made me feel insulted. I felt like nothing more than a clerk. This way of teaching seemed to be built around the premise that the teacher only got in the way of students' lock-step progress through a list of reading and writing skills. Teachers' professional decision-making was ignored; children's learning capabilities weren't respected. It was the ultimate "drill-and-kill" program, where skills were presented in isolation without any context.

For instance, sequence was taught by asking students to look at pictures and place them in order. It sounds logical, until you think of the many children like Francesca, a developing reader from a busy family, all of whom worked or went to school. I asked her to talk to me about why she sequenced things the way she did on her skills sheet. The card had four pictures—one showed a sink with dishes in the drainer, one a woman cooking, another a family sitting at the table, and the last a picture of dirty dishes. Francesca had chosen the dirty dishes pic-ture for the first frame. In our conversation, she told me that at home she or her brother would have to wash the dishes first before dinner could be served. Obviously, in this student's worldview, putting the dirty dishes first was accurate.

This situation, along with many others, helped me realize that I needed to turn away from skill builders and toward enriching stories with other examples of text. The texts my students were reading were too limited—again, an insult—so it was up to me to help them find texts that interested, challenged, and excited them. Perhaps Individual Learning Packets would be a way.

Of course, I had to deal with reality. Would my principal balk at my requisi-tions for manila envelopes to house the packets? What about the photocopying of single poems or short stories? What about my request for a typewriter in the classroom? I must admit I became ready to do battle to see that the classroom would work for the students.

My principal gave me less of a fight than I expected. Since he received a lot of "stuff" in manila envelopes from Central Office, he agreed to hold onto the better ones and send them my way. Also, our district holds a yard sale each year, during which old equipment is offered to the public to purchase. I asked my principal to keep an eye out for a workable typewriter. He noticed one listed on the items to be sold, explained that he had a teacher who was planning a writing corner and that a typewriter would be helpful for students whose muscle control made clear handwriting difficult, and gained the support of the depart-ment chair, who was in charge. In fact, this person said he had an old electric that would probably be even better. When I called to thank him, he mentioned that the library was being converted to a computer system and that the card cat-alog would be cleared out. Perhaps I could use the recycled cards? I contacted the head librarian, who said he would be glad to hold onto the cards that weren't yet thrown away. Since I was determined to optimize the learning experience for my students, I was not bashful about seeking help from others. For the most part, people were eager to help, and if they didn't have what I needed, they could often give helpful suggestions of where I might go next. By being an advo-cate for all my students, I found a community that would support them in their learning.

Ah, but decisions, decisions! I had originally planned, I'm almost sorry to admit now, to use the packets only with my academically gifted students, and

Students develop an understanding of and respect for diversity in lan-guage use, patterns, and dialects across cultures, ethnic groups, geo-graphic regions, and social roles.

those who were "functioning above and beyond" our basic reading program. I did create the units for them, but to my surprise, "less proficient" readers soon asked if they could use the packets as well. So, we all began to develop material that was thematically connected to their reading—stories, activities that encouraged research, reading of different genres, writing for a variety of purposes, and presentations that could be done with the whole group, with small groups, or one on one. Soon, the students demanded specific learning packets on topics they wanted to know more about, and they began to create their own.

As the students continued to develop their packets, I was able to help them use the tools of research with not one groan of "Why do we have to do this?" For example, they discovered that, in order to share their packets with others, they needed to write down source information, so I gave a minilesson on bibliography. I've found that younger students love to use bibliography cards, so giving them a reason to put the cards to use was readily accepted. This way, students had actual, firsthand copies of title, author, and subject library catalog cards. They learned how the information on each was organized differently because of its proposed use. Another surprise: it wasn't long before one of the students offered to organize our own classroom library using a modified system of the card catalog. Another student developed a chart for how to go about finding information outside the classroom; when the kids were finished with what research they could in the classroom, they looked at Brian's "Where to Look Next" chart. It had a magnifying glass to play up the concept of looking closely, and consisted of a list of references located in the school and public libraries. Yet another student, who was working with a special needs classmate, liked Brian's idea and thought his buddy would benefit from a chart that was called "How to Get Started," and so he and the buddy created one. A "can-do" attitude caught hold in the classroom.

The students had taken over the curriculum; it was exciting to see them actively engaged in their learning and provide the makings of a classroom culture to allow this to take place. All they needed was the permission to do so, the room in which to do it, and an atmosphere that was safe and that encouraged and rewarded risk taking.

Students read a wide range of print and nonprint texts to build an understanding of texts, of themselves, and of the cultures of the United States and the world; to acquire new information; to respond to the needs and demands of society and the workplace; and for personal fulfillment. Among these texts are fiction and nonfiction, classic and contemporary works.

Students adjust their use of spoken, written, and visual language (e.g., conventions, style, vocabulary) to communicate effectively with a variety of audiences and for different purposes.

Organizing Groups

I didn't just start groups out of the blue. After I initially learned about them at the "Literature and the Creative Self" seminar, I knew I needed to learn even more so that I could understand how what I was doing supported learner-centered principles and encouraged democracy in the classroom. I did a lot of reading and observing; seeing groups of real students grappling with working together was very helpful. My overall purpose for wanting to have students work in groups was twofold: (1) in smaller, more intimate settings, students who might need extra support from teams would be able to receive it—groups would be a place for practicing new learning strategies and developing confidence; and (2) students would be able to discover their individual strengths and learn how to put them to use with different strengths that others had to offer—for example,

Students participate as knowledgeable, reflective, creative, and critical members of a variety of literacy communities.

students would learn how to practice leadership skills as well as how to work with others, and those who might be loners because they sensed they were "different" would learn how to become part of something.

I feel strongly that I need to help students know that I believe in them as learners. One way for me to do this is through affirmations—positive statements that may be quotations from authors, civic or cultural leaders, or other well-known and not-so-well-known individuals. Two affirmations that have proved to be important in our community are "You become successful by helping others be successful," and "Your hard work does not go unnoticed. Thank you for your effort. It is appreciated." I try to "catch" students when they're demonstrating positive behaviors, such as sincerely complimenting a fellow group member for his or her participation, and I make sure to point out what I've noticed. If I observe a student getting fidgety, I will often say, "You've done a fine job of being patient, and we'll be moving to small groups in a minute." Then I keep to that timeframe, because that student needs to know I'm living up to my end of the commitment—he or she will give me undivided attention for one minute, and I will make sure that after that minute is over students will indeed gather into their groups.

I have developed different ways to help my students understand group process. Sometimes they work through a direct approach; other times through a more inductive one. To determine which will work best I try to help based on what I know about the students in the class. If they've never worked in groups before or have had bad group experiences, then I will walk them through the strategies that make groups successful. For example, I was working with some students on developing interpretive questions that they would later use to conduct reading discussion groups. They needed guidance in developing and sharing the questions, so I helped show

what the process would be. We began by discussing "Jack and the Beanstalk," and talked about how the story had been written in many different versions. Then we took the copies of the version we had and read them to ourselves during silent reading time. After we had had the chance to complete our reading, we moved into our discussion groups. I said, "Think about the story. In your group write down some 'why' questions you might have about it, and decide on one you'd like to share with the class."

The groups went to work, using different approaches. After ten minutes, I asked them to begin to decide on which question they'd like to share, and the discussions that followed quickly became impassioned. The class came together after another ten minutes, and as we talked we discovered that one group still hadn't come up with their decision:

Me: Why do you suppose you were unable to choose?

Brian: Everybody wanted their own.

Sonia: Yeah. No one would back down.

Me: How about the other groups? How did you decide?

Roshan: We chose, but we all didn't really want the question. Justin made us choose his. He kept bugging us till we gave in.

Towanna: We decided on one, but two of us had it so we figured it was a good one.

Me: What about the other two groups?

Dashone: We didn't get it done because we were voting.

Brian: We decided, but it took a long time.

Me: Why did it take a long time?

Brian: We kept talking about different ones, and if it wasn't really a "why" question, we decided not to use it.

Me: So, what would you do differently?

Brian: Check earlier.

Me: Let's look at the way your groups worked. What did you do that helped the group decide on a question?

Dashone: We shouldn't vote.

Me: Why?

Dashone: Because voting means someone loses. George felt kind of bad. Alicia felt bad too. So no voting!

Roshan: We chose our question because Justin kept bugging us to choose his.

Justin: But it was the only "why" question. You have to follow directions, you know.

Roshan: But you didn't even listen to Mike's or Lara's.

Lara: So you have to give each person a chance.

Mike: Yeah. And for some of us to write as fast.

Me: What do we have so far here?

Roshan: Take turns. See if we're following directions.

Brian: You might have to give up your question. Otherwise you won't get it done.

Me: Good, specific actions! Those are the kinds of actions a manager might take. It sounds like Justin's group didn't check to understand if everyone knew what a "why" question is. It sounds as if they could have used a leader, a person in the group who makes sure everyone gets a chance.

Towanna: We decided on a question, but no one had paper to write it down. I would say we needed someone like that.

Another way to help students understand working together is a concept I call "entering the fish bowl." One group goes to the center of the class and processes their task, while the rest of the class observes how effectively the group uses strategies. We note the strategies—asking questions in order to understand, making sure everyone participates, summarizing for the group, making sure that the group uses its time effectively, for instance—and give feedback regarding our observations. Members of the group also process their perceptions of their group's effectiveness by filling out group evaluation sheets. I sit in on discussions after the sheets are filled out, and we work through comments. We talk about the purpose of the task, we work out concerns, and we talk about what works, what doesn't, and why. During the year, students have the opportunity to select their own groupings, and we reflect on how effective those groupings are. I quite often hear "We're too good friends to do work together," and the next time self-selection occurs, that judgment is taken into account. For example, one group realized they were too easily distracted by their social agenda, and asked if they could break into two smaller groups rather than intrude on other groups already established. This is the kind of self-management I hope my students will take with them and put to good use throughout their lives.

It's important that groups learn to monitor themselves and know what they need to do, even if there is no one person assigned to the responsibility. More than anything, the tasks given to groups have to be organized. The paper, the glue, the markers or scissors, whatever the group will need, must be in good order. I float about the room as the groups work, and I observe closely. If students have difficulty in pacing, I talk to them about creating a project timeline, but I avoid rescuing them; I let them struggle with a solution by saying, "Give it a try and decide if it works." As they have more experience in solving their problems, it's important they have the opportunity to refer to previous strategies and review them to see if they'll fit into their current discussion.

Evaluation of Group Interaction

				Notes
Participation:	Did everyone participate?	Y	N	
	Did everyone give at least one response?	Y	N	
Preparation:	Was everyone prepared?	Y	N	
	Did students use notes or refer to the reading?	Y	N	
	Did any group member refer directly to the material?	Y	N	
	Did they cite or read anything?	Y	N	
Getting the Job Done:	Did the group reach its goal?	Y	N	
	Did members make consensus statements?	Y	N	
	Did students try to answer any "whys"?	Y	N	
Atmosphere:	Was the group cooperative and friendly in the spirit of working toward understanding?	Y	N	

Connecting the Students' Learning through Presentations

Because I feel it's important for students to own their learning, I encourage them to present their knowledge to others in new ways. Some questions I ask them to ask themselves include the following:

* What have I discovered that has made the greatest impact on me?
* What has affected me the most?
* How do I feel about what I have learned?
* How can I share that with the others?

To prepare them for sharing effectively with others, I introduce them to successful presentation strategies by giving them handouts on preparing videos, writing research reports, using photos to step into different time periods, using drama to make their presentations come to life, and creating exhibits. I sometimes demonstrate certain presentation formats myself; I sometimes show videos of presentations; we sometimes all listen to audiotapes (tapes of professional or student radio talk or news shows, for instance, can help children conceptualize how to interview others or how to present complicated information in a succinct, clear format). I also share ways that other students have worked through their ideas to create successful projects. Some of the projects the students have come up with include an underwater submarine, an uncharted mine, and even a setting for a "Star Trek" episode. They have used a number of different resources in a variety of meaningful ways, and the knowledge they have gained far surpasses what I thought might be possible.

Helping All Students Value Different Voices

Throughout the year, I spend a great deal of time letting students know that I expect them to do well and that I will not ask them to do anything that they cannot be successful with at some level. Two activities that my students have consistently named as not liking at first but eventually enjoying and learning from are their "Getting to Know Me" pieces and their reading journals.

"Auto-Bio" Poems

Each year, we create "Auto-Bio," or "Getting to Know Me" poems–poems that tell others about ourselves so we can get to know one another through playful language and metaphor. Students are often hesitant at first— the classroom community is not yet established, and trust is a major issue. Unfortunately, many children learn at a very early age that to divulge parts of their lives and cultures is to risk being mocked for who they are, and this hurts deeply. They learn to cover up their uniqueness in order to conform and "fit in," but by playing safe, they risk losing not only their voices but their sense of self. This is a deep-seated and difficult process to begin to reverse, but I have seen time and again how providing a foundation for a respectful environment and encouraging students to speak in their own voices affects and changes them in powerful, positive ways.

The Reading Journal

The reading journal is actually a combination of reader response and classroom management. The day after a daily reading assignment, students bring a question to class about what they've read. During reading time, they write in their journals to reflect on and respond to passages, and I read through the questions they've written down. This usually takes about five to seven minutes. I ask students to share their responses if they want to, and I try to encourage those who might otherwise remain silent. Once one student starts, others usually follow in rapid succession until all responses have been discussed. I then ask if anyone would like to share a question, and the rest of the class is invited to respond to it. During this part of the discussion, students call on one another to check out how others are processing the questions they asked. After this exchange, they might move into small groups to discuss what they read, what they heard, and what they felt about the reading. Each group then reports on what they've discovered.

The students tell me that they don't worry if they don't "get" the reading on their own, because they know that by the end of the class discussion they will.

Auto-Bio Poem

Follow the pattern below to create an eleven-line auto-bio poem that will introduce you to your classmates. Be creative! Design a poster or collage and place a copy of your poem in the middle.

Line 1:	[Your first name]	Martha
Line 2:	[Four descriptive traits]	Hard-working, caring, loyal, curious
Line 3:	Sibling of . . .	Mike, Stephanie, Jerry, Mary, Tim, Rebecca, Julian Anthony, and Lisa
Line 4:	Lover of [people, ideas] . . .	books, volleyball, teaching, and learning
Line 5:	Who feels . . .	happiest with Nathanial
Line 6:	Who needs . . .	a pat on the back once in a while
Line 7:	Who gives . . .	friendship, encouragement, and smiles
Line 8:	Who fears . . .	unhappiness, pain, and winter
Line 9:	Who would like to see . . .	a celebration of acceptance and tolerance for all
Line 10:	Resident of [your city] . . .	Urbana
Line 11:	[Your last name]	Sierra-Perry!

Students develop an understanding of and respect for diversity in language use, patterns, and dialects across cultures, ethnic groups, geographic regions, and social roles.

Students apply a wide range of strategies to comprehend, interpret, evaluate, and appreciate texts. They draw on their prior experience, their interactions with other readers and writers, their knowledge of word meaning and other texts, their word identification strategies, and their understanding of textual features (e.g., sound-letter correspondence, sentence structure, context, graphics).

Also, I've heard often that they like the "what they heard and what they felt" parts of their discussions. Students whose first language is other than English benefit from the different ways they feel invited into the conversation and the extra time spent discussing ideas, and native speakers certainly benefit from communicating in different ways to those from other cultures, and in turn understanding the text in ways they might not have otherwise. This kind of learning is immeasurably valuable not only in the classroom but in the context of the children's lives, present and future.

Perspectives of Other Cultures

Another part of helping students to value different voices is to involve them on a regular basis with books that reflect the perspectives of different members of our American culture. Instead of only a "Group of the Month" type of salute, the curriculum needs to speak to students throughout the year. When I initially struggled with the idea of including multicultural and gender perspectives (and I did struggle!), I asked myself two questions that still stay with me:

- How can I enrich the classroom experience by being more inclusive? (I knew it went beyond simply adding more books by women and members of various cultures.)
- Why should students want to know about the perspectives of other groups?

Sometimes you have to revisit your own roots. My father has an expression he uses when he sees one person denigrate another—"We're all brothers and sisters under the skin!"—and this expression is an internal reminder that kicks in when I find myself dealing with a difficult person in a difficult situation; it helps me when I'm tempted to respond in a quick, judgmental way.

So, once again I looked outside myself to find professional experience to help me develop my pedagogy more clearly. The National Endowment for the Humanities offered a summer seminar entitled "Reinterpretations of American Literature," and again I was fortunate to attend and learn. For me, the question was to find a way to use literature to show how our common humanity connects us rather than creates divisiveness and estrangement. Incredibly, during the seminar I read my first book by a Latino author: *Bless Me, Ultima,* by Rudolfo A. Anaya. My immediate family had essentially been assimilated within the dominant culture, but during my early childhood we had lived with my grandparents and were in close contact with uncles and aunts, and this experience helped me feel at ease with the book's cadence and mystical aspects. Others in the class cited these features as being difficult for them to understand on an intuitive level. I connected this with my own teaching and with my students—how difficult it must be for those of different cultures to relate to and engage in books or stories that might have a point of view and way of understanding the world quite different from their own; how blind I had been to that, and how I had therefore not adapted my teaching to reach them.

These insights also made me realize that I had shortchanged students from our dominant, white, middle-class culture as well—think of how difficult it must have been for them to understand the language of Louisa May Alcott, for instance, since I had neglected to provide a scaffold that would tell them something about the time in which she wrote as well as about the circumstances in her life that might have influenced her way of perceiving her world. It was my responsibility to guide them with different reading strategies. Students are often

Students apply a wide range of strategies to comprehend, interpret, evaluate, and appreciate texts. They draw on their prior experience, their interactions with other readers and writers, their knowledge of word meaning and other texts, their word identification strategies, and their understanding of textual features (e.g., sound-letter correspondence, sentence structure, context, graphics).

unfamiliar with an author's use of language, diction, and style, whether that author is writing from a different culture, a different time, or simply a different frame of reference, and we must enrich their worlds by showing them the many possibilities of story. The various perspectives that authors have taken and continue to take on the human condition connect us on a very powerful emotional level, and I wanted to remember that always so that my students could experience it.

This insight led me to study more and take more workshops on multicultural issues. It also led to my speaking up at grade-level meetings and district language arts curriculum meetings. I found that other teachers were making a similar journey, so we worked together to have a professor from our local university provide informational presentations and workshops on using multicultural materials in our classrooms.

The question that always guides me when we read is, "Is this only part of the story?" Of course, it usually is, especially for those of us who must still use anthologies or basals in our classrooms. Therefore, any time we encounter issues such as slavery and oppression (which come up in every fifth-grade classroom when we study some areas of American history) I make sure we cover all different points of view so the students can reach a clear, rich understanding of what it means to be human. That way, I hope my students will gain insight into other perspectives on a deep level so that they grow into responsible, caring adults in a very complicated society. The main principle that drives our curriculum is that in order for students to move forward, we all need to reconcile differences and move on to the "justice for all" egalitarian climate we foster in our classroom.

Stepping Back and Looking In: Still in the Process of Becoming a Teacher

As I review the NCTE/IRA Standards for the English Language Arts, I find that the experiences in this book's classrooms do address them, and my hope is that you as the reader gain insight and ideas for your own classroom practices. Some common themes reflected both in the standards and in these teachers' classrooms appear over and over again. Students are constructing meaning. The social nature of learning and communication is recognized, and, more important, brought into play in the classroom. Students are expected to see one another as resources and assistants to discuss works in progress, in order to gain further understanding. There is a blend of direct instruction and student response in the classroom. There is a great deal of "just in time" instruction, when a student needs to be introduced to a strategy, a skill, a text, and that is when these teachers try to do it, no matter what the "it" is at the moment. In order to be able to teach this way, however, we must be prepared and continue to prepare ourselves for those teachable moments. We must orchestrate our classrooms so that the questions raised are robust, and we can only do this by keeping ourselves involved professionally as well as by reviewing our teaching practice reflectively. We need to remind ourselves of interdisciplinary connections in order to reach as many of our students as possible, and we need to communicate with them in a variety of formats—records, tapes (audio and video), news clips, art pieces, "experts," artifacts, and the like. As we work through our planning, it helps us to have road maps that we can follow in order to find the best ways to teach *all* of our students.

Never underestimate the power of sharing professional questions with colleagues; it is perhaps the most important way to reflect meaningfully about our teaching. During each of my National Endowment for the Humanities experiences, I was required to keep a journal, and my professors responded to my questions. My writing about what I was trying to do in the classroom helped me to conceptualize my actions, and when my professor responded I was able to gain more insight into why I wanted to do what I wanted to do. He would probe for further reflection from me and also show me how my reflections were connected to our class discussions and readings. As I communicated with Deb Foertsch, Jan Ewing, and Stephanie Sierra, the other teachers in this book, I found myself following my professor's model and using probes to help them conceptualize their teaching behaviors so that I could understand them more deeply. I think we all gained from the interaction. I hope to continue our conversations, because I have learned a great deal about myself as a teacher and thinker. And I still keep that journal!

Some Final Thoughts about Standards

Just as the artisans described at the beginning of this book saw a perfect, apparently finished urn as only a stage along the way to an even more priceless work of art, we can see the NCTE/IRA Standards for the English Language Arts not as perfect and immutable but as a stage on the way to the locally crafted standards that will serve each community's needs and goals. I have worked on state committees to develop standards, outcomes, and assessments, and I participate because I want to be sure that they are as fair to students as possible. In some classrooms in my state (as I'm sure is common in every state), students have not been given equal opportunity to participate in a rich curriculum; with the implementation of our state assessment program, our school district determined that all students needed this enriched curriculum in order even to be assessed. So, chapter teachers, ESL teachers, and special education teachers all became players as we updated our curriculum. They were introduced to assessment instruments that would be used, and because of their expertise in working with adapting the curriculum, *all* teachers and students benefited. I hope I continue to see such ongoing opportunities, rather than immutable plans that cannot respond to students' needs. As long as we all continue to be involved as professionals, amazing things can happen. The best part is that the students take off in ways we could never anticipate. And isn't that what it's all about?

References and Resources for Further Reading

American Psychological Task Force on Psychology in Education and the Mid-continent. (1992). *Learner-centered psychological principles: Guidelines for school reform.* Aurora, CO: McREL.

Anaya, R. A. (1972). *Bless me, Ultima: A novel.* Berkeley, CA: TQS.

Anderson, P. M. (Ed.). (1993). *English language arts and the at-risk student.* Schenectady: New York State English Council.

Armstrong, T. (1994). *Multiple intelligences in the classroom.* Alexandria, VA: Association for Supervision and Curriculum Development.

Darling-Hammond, L. (1994). Performance-based assessment and educational equity. *Harvard Educational Review, 64* (1), 5–30.

Flores, B. (1990, August). *Breaking the deficit myths of diverse children's language and culture.* Bellringer session at Whole Language Umbrella Conference "Perspectives on Whole Language Past, Present, Potential," St. Louis, Missouri. (Cassette Recording). High Ridge, MO: Network Communications.

Fox, S. (1990, August). *Implementing the "different" philosophy regarding diverse children's language and culture.* Bellringer Session at Whole Language Umbrella Conference "Perspectives on Whole Language Past, Present, Potential," St. Louis, Missouri. (Cassette Recording). High Ridge, MO: Network Communications.

Glasser, W. (1992). *The quality school: Managing students without coercion* (2nd ed.). New York: HarperPerennial.

Introduction to shared inquiry, An. (1992). Chicago: Great Books Foundation.

Johnson, D. W., Johnson, R. T., and Holubec, E. J. (1994). *The new circles of learning: Cooperation in the classroom and school.* Alexandria, VA: Association for Supervision and Curriculum Development.

Marzano, R. J. (1992). *A different kind of classroom: Teaching with dimensions of learning.* Alexandria, VA: Association for Supervision and Curriculum Development.

Pearson, D. (1994, January). Standards for the English language arts: A policy perspective. *Journal of Reading Behavior, 25* (4), 457–475.

Resnick, L. B., and Klopfer, L. E. (Eds.). (1989). *Toward the thinking curriculum: Current cognitive research.* 1989 ASCD Yearbook. Alexandria, VA: Association for Supervision and Curriculum Development.

Rose, M. (1991, July 3). Education standards must be reclaimed for democratic ends. *Chronicle of Higher Education,* p. A32.

Singer, D. G., and Revenson, T. A. (1978). *A Piaget primer: How a child thinks.* New York: New American Library.

Slavin, R. E. (1987). *Cooperative learning: Student teams* (2nd ed.). Washington, DC: National Education Association.

Slavin, R. E., Sharan, S., Kagan, S., Hertz-Lazarowitz., R., Webb, C., and Schmuck, R. (Eds.). (1985). *Learning to cooperate, cooperating to learn.* New York: Plenum.

Sizer, T. R. (1984). *Horace's compromise: The dilemma of the American high school.* Boston, MA: Houghton Mifflin.

Sizer, T. R. (1992). *Horace's school: Redesigning the high school.* Boston, MA: Houghton Mifflin.

Spritzer, D. R. (Ed.). (1993, Spring). Teaching the language arts to gifted and talented students [Special issue]. *Oregon English Journal, 15* (1).

Stepien, W., and Gallagher, S. (1993, April). Problem-based learning: As authentic as it gets. *Educational Leadership, 50* (7), 25–28.

Stiggins, R. J. (1994). *Student-centered classroom assessment.* New York: Merrill.

AUTHOR

Martha Sierra-Perry has been in education for over twenty years. Her first teaching position was at Kelly Avenue Grade School in Peoria Heights, Illinois. She later taught at Franklin Junior High/Middle School in Champaign, Illinois. She presently teaches English at Centennial High School. In addition to seventeen years of classroom experience, she has been Director of Secondary Curriculum for Champaign Schools and principal of Jefferson Middle School in Champaign.

She was named "Outstanding Teacher" by the Centennial PTSA, and the "Principal's Award" was established in her honor at Parkland Community College to create a scholarship for middle school students to attend the "College for Kids Program." She has been the recipient of National Endowment for the Humanities Grants, and was selected to attend Harvard University's Principal Center for Leadership.

At the state level, she has served on the Illinois Goal Assessment Program Advisory Committee, Language Arts Advisory Committee, and Writing Assessment Committee. This past summer she served on a committee to develop an integrated reading rubric for assessment. She currently serves as co-chair for the language arts section of the Illinois Academic Standards Project.

Marty has been a member of NCTE since 1969 as a student at Illinois State University. She is also a member of the Association for Supervision and Curriculum Development, Phi Delta Kappa, and Delta Kappa Gamma.

Her professional interests include integrating technology into the classroom, classroom assessment, and working on University of Illinois committees on gender and minorities and the improvement of programs for prospective teachers, especially for prospective English Language Arts teachers. Her community interests include serving as a board member on the YWCA to pursue its mission to empower women and eradicate racism.

For fun, Marty enjoys time with her family, "surfing the Net," reading with her son Nathanial, and sister weekends. She lives in Urbana with her husband, Ed, and Nathanial.

CONTRIBUTORS

Jan Ewing is currently a second-grade teacher at Cherokee School in Lake Forest and a lecturer in education at Lake Forest College, Illinois. She earned a master's degree in educational leadership and administration at National-Louis University and has taught and served as a consultant for fifteen years at the elementary level and eight years at the college level. Her interests include parent involvement in education and interdisciplinary instruction, both topics on which she has written and presented staff development programs. Giving children choices and opportunities for responsible decision making is an area of continual advocacy. Jan has great belief in the abilities of all children and all learners. She has also served as a school improvement team member, secretary and president of her district's PTA, and a parent volunteer in her home school district. Jan is an avid reader of adult and children's literature, a writer, and a roving amateur photographer.

Deborah Foertsch has been a teacher for seventeen years. Almost all of those years have been at fourth- and fifth-grade levels in self-contained classrooms. She taught at Eastlawn School, Rantoul, Illinois, for ten years and is currently at Carrie Busey School, Champaign, Illinois. Deb is active in professional organizations such as Phi Delta Kappa, Delta Kappa Gamma, and the Reading Council, both local and state. Within her district, she serves as Fifth Grade Level Chairperson for Champaign Schools, as well as being active on district committees for curriculum and assessment. This past summer she participated in the National Center for Supercomputing Applications Resource for Science Education Program. Deb has been awarded a local television station's "Golden Apple Award" and an "Excellence in Education" award from the State of Illinois. Her professional interests include integrating technology into the classroom and keeping up with and enjoying children's literature. For fun, Deb is a member of a book club and serves as an adviser for an after-school student newspaper at her school.

Stephanie Sierra has taught for twenty-one years. A 1973 graduate of Illinois State University, where she also earned a master's degree in education in 1980, Stephanie has taught in grades 2, 3, 4, and 6, first at Tioga School in Bensonville, Illinois, then in Peoria, Illinois, at Holy Family Catholic School, and for the last fifteen years at Oakwood School in Elyria, Ohio. In 1988 Stephanie founded a TAWL (Teachers Applying Whole Language) group in Elyria, and in 1993 spearheaded the first Language Alive Conference, which has featured nationally renowned children's authors and educators, as well as regionally recognized teachers. She has served as president and vice-president of the Network of Erie Shore Teachers of English and Language Arts (NESTELA), the NCTE affiliate for Lorain County, Ohio, and is a trustee of the Center for Leadership and Education, an education planning and resource asset in north central Ohio. Stephanie reports that her most rewarding career experience was having a former student write, "I want to go into teaching and be a teacher like you."

Other Books from NCTE Related to English Language Arts Content Standards

Standards for the English Language Arts

From the National Council of Teachers of English and the International Reading Association

What should English language arts students know and be able to do? This book—the culmination of more than three years of intense research and discussion among members of the English language arts teaching community, parents, and policymakers—answers this question by presenting standards that encompass the use of print, oral, and visual language and addresses six interrelated English language arts: reading, writing, speaking, listening, viewing, and visually representing. *Standards for the English Language Arts* starts by examining the rationale for standard setting—why NCTE and IRA believe defining standards is important and what we hope to accomplish by doing so. The book then explores the assumptions that underlie the standards, defines and elaborates each standard individually, and provides real-life classroom vignettes in which readers can glimpse standards in practice. Designed to complement state and local standards efforts, this document will help educators prepare *all* K–12 students for the literacy demands of the twenty-first century. 1996. Grades K–12. ISBN 0-8141-4676-7.
Stock No. 46767-4025
$18.00 nonmembers, $13.00 NCTE members

Standards Consensus Series

Books in this series serve as useful guides for K–12 teachers who are striving to align lively, classroom-tested practices with standards. A survey of local, state, and national documents revealed a broad consensus in the key topics most frequently addressed in standards; clearly local conditions may vary, but English language arts teachers across the country face many common challenges as they help students meet higher literacy standards. These first releases in the Standards Consensus Series draw on these common threads and bring together the best teaching ideas from prior NCTE publications in topical books with practical, everyday applications in the classroom. Among the titles available:

Teaching the Writing Process in High School (ISBN 0-8141-5286-4)
Stock No. 52864-4025
$12.95 nonmembers, $9.95 NCTE members

Teaching Literature in High School: The Novel (ISBN 0-8141-5282-1)
Stock No. 52821-4025
$12.95 nonmembers, $9.95 NCTE members

Teaching Literature in Middle School: Fiction (ISBN 0-8141-5285-6)
Stock No. 52856-4025
$12.95 nonmembers; $9.95 NCTE members

Motivating Writing in Middle School (ISBN 0-8141-5287-2)
Stock No. 52872-4025
$12.95 nonmembers, $9.95 NCTE members

Additional Titles in the Standards in Practice Series

Standards in Practice, Grades K–2 by Linda K. Crafton (ISBN 0-8141-4691-0)
Stock No. 46910-4025
$15.95 nonmembers, $11.95 NCTE members

Standards in Practice, Grades 6–8 by Jeffrey D. Wilhelm (ISBN 0-8141-4694-5)
Stock No. 46945-4025
$15.95 nonmembers, $11.95 NCTE members

Standards in Practice, Grades 9–12 by Peter Smagorinsky (ISBN 0-8141-4695-3)
Stock No. 46953-4025
$15.95 nonmembers, $11.95 NCTE members

Ordering Information

Any of the useful resources described above can be ordered from the National Council of Teachers of English by phoning 1-800-369-6283; by faxing your order to 1-217-328-9645; by e-mailing your order request to <orders@ncte.org>; or by sending your order to NCTE Order Fulfillment, 1111 W. Kenyon Road, Urbana, IL 61801-1096.

To preview these resources, visit the NCTE home page at <http://www.ncte.org>.

DATE DUE